Dedicated

To my husband, my family, my many students and my friends who shared their ideas and encouraged me to write this new book.

Joan Toole

Cooking En Concert with Microwave

Blending the best of both cooking worlds with your microwave oven, the Maid in the Kitchen.

Another cookbook by Joan Toole is *Cooking With Microwave Magic*, a book of techniques, recipes and menus for those new to microwave cooking.

Library of Congress Catalog Card
Number 79-54854
ISBN 0-9603418-0-3
Printed 1979

Acknowledgements

Designed and edited by Art and
Design, Hayward, California

Illustrations by Ruth Neptune

Photography by Steve Gerber

Front cover photograph by
George Selland

Food Stylist, Stevie Bass

Diet consultation, J. Gerald Toole, M.D.

Special thanks to Phyllis Larsen,
author of Ghirardelli Original
Chocolate Cookbook

Special thanks to Lois Frazee

Table of Contents

About
The
Author

Joan Toole, author and leading San Francisco Bay Area expert in the culinary art of microwave cooking, introduces her new book, *Cooking En Concert With Microwave*. This book adds new dimensions to the basic concepts of microwave cookery.

In her previous book, *Cooking With Microwave Magic*, Joan emphasizes the basic techniques that are essential for achieving outstanding results in microwave cooking. That book is now in its third printing.

In this new book, Joan emphasizes cooking **en concert**. This technique utilizes the microwave oven with the cooktop, conventional oven or barbecue to take advantage of the best features of these appliances while preparing food in record time. Joan also tells how to adapt old favorite recipes to the microwave oven.

She has appeared many times on Bay Area television shows and has been a featured speaker at the San Francisco Energy Exposition and the San Francisco International Gourmet and Wine Festival. Joan is currently conducting weekly microwave cooking classes throughout the Bay Area.

Joan is a graduate of Oregon State University with a degree in Home Economics. She is a member of the American Home Economics Association, the Home Economists in Business, and the International Microwave Power Institute. As a busy and successful career woman, Joan finds that her microwave oven is truly her maid in the kitchen. She resides in San Jose, California, with her husband and three sons.

Joan Toole

Introduction

Let's cook **En Concert!** The versatility of the microwave oven enables it truly to take its place as your maid in the kitchen.

In this book you will find many ways to use this "maid"—from ideas for meals in minutes to elegant meals in half the usual cooking time.

My first book, COOKING WITH MICROWAVE MAGIC, emphasizes the basic techniques of microwave cooking and presents the fundamentals for using the microwave oven. In this book I have added new dimensions to these basic concepts.

To take full advantage of the microwave oven, it is essential that one have an understanding of Timing, After-cooking and Rotating and Stirring. I call these the THREE KEYS TO SUCCESS. An explanation of the importance of each is found in the THREE KEYS TO SUCCESS chapter.

I have divided this book into three sections.

Section I contains many recipes in which the microwave oven is used **en concert** with conventional kitchen appliances. In addition to many wonderful, tasty dishes which can be micro-cooked on a daily basis for the family, I have included elegant entrees for those special occasions. Using the microwave oven, the cooking times for these are amazingly fast.

Section II features those dishes in which the microwave oven can shine as your maid in the kitchen. Here we have main dishes, vegetables, desserts, sauces, egg cookery and super sandwiches. All are delicious, easy and quick.

Section III is devoted to specialty aspects of microwave cooking. I have included recipes for those who are interested in weight-watching or who are on low-cholesterol, low-fat or low-sodium diets. I would like to express my appreciation for the advice and expertise in the Diet Cookery chapter to J. Gerald Toole, M.D., a leading cardiac rehabilitation specialist. He is Director, Cardiac Rehabilitation Program, Santa Clara Valley Medical Center and Clinical Associate Professor of Medicine, Stanford University School of Medicine.

In addition, you will find the QUICK TIP chapter in Section III to be invaluable in making your microwave oven a pleasure to use. Here I have accumulated tips which can be applied to many dishes and uses of the microwave oven. They cover many situations and, therefore, should be reviewed from time to time to take full advantage of them.

THREE
KEYS TO
SUCCESS

Your success with the microwave oven will be assured if you remember the principle of this form of cooking and use the KEYS TO SUCCESS given throughout this book. **What is the basic principle of microwave cooking?—Waves of energy from the megatron cause the molecules of the food to move rapidly against each other. This rapid movement causes friction, which causes heat within the food. There is enough internal heat generated to cook the food. The pattern of the waves of energy is changed somewhat by the shape and size of the cooking container and the food being cooked. When the food is removed from the microwave oven the internal heat does not stop immediately, but the food continues to cook for a time as the heated molecules slow to their normal rate of movement.**

The quick cooking made possible by microwave energy leads to three practical KEYS TO SUCCESS. **If you keep these KEYS TO SUCCESS in mind you will use your microwave oven to its fullest potential.**

Timing

Always cook food the minimum length of time given in the recipe. Test to see if it is cooked to your satisfaction. If not, cook for a few seconds or minutes more, depending upon the food, and then test again.

After-cooking

Once the cooking cycle has been completed, the food will continue to cook for a period of time. Allow food to rest until the molecules within the food slow down. The amount of time will vary depending on the type of food.

Rotating and Stirring

Microwave energy is reflected by the sides, top and bottom of the oven, so cooking is not completely even. To insure even cooking, however, you must rotate the cooking container and stir the food more than you would in conventional cooking.

Note: When using variable power you do not have to rotate and stir as frequently.

Continued on next page 17

With these 3 KEYS TO SUCCESS you can open the way to successful microwave cooking. How do you use these KEYS TO SUCCESS in your kitchen?—I shall discuss each one separately in this section and remind you of them as we go along.

TIMING

Proper timing is the major KEY TO SUCCESS with the microwave oven. Until you become familiar with your oven and know just how long it takes to cook food to the doneness that you like, **start with the minimum cooking time given in the recipe. If further cooking is needed, add a few seconds or a minute or two at a time. It is worth the effort for, as in any cooking, once food is overdone, it is overdone forever.**

The times mentioned in this book are based on a microwave oven of 600 to 675 "cooking power" watts. Microwave ovens with lower cooking watts will take longer. Cooking times vary with the type of food being cooked. Space is provided in this book for you to record the cooking times that you find best for your microwave oven.

You will soon get to know the length of time needed for the foods you most often cook. Keep this book and a pencil by your microwave oven. **Write down the time required to cook your favorites, noting the starting temperature in the spaces provided in the following pages.** Before long you will have a long list of the foods your family likes.

Starting Temperature. The temperature of the food before starting to cook it affects the cooking time considerably. **The colder the starting temperature, the longer the cooking time.** When you use a new recipe, notice the starting temperature for the ingredients and adjust your times accordingly. Reheating a serving takes 15 to 30 seconds less time when you start at room temperature.

For example, a cup of cold mashed potatoes takes 1 to 1½ minutes while a cup of cold scalloped potatoes takes 2 to 2½ minutes. A dinner plate of food takes 30 to 45 seconds from room temperature, 45 to 60 seconds from the refrigerator.

Roasts directly from the refrigerator take 30 seconds per pound more time to cook than one already at room temperature. For example, a 4-pound beef roast, if from the refrigerator, would take 30 minutes to reach medium doneness instead of the usual 28 minutes. Frozen roasts require 60 seconds per pound more time to cook. **More**

18

details on defrosting foods are given in the Quick-Tips Section.

Moisture Content. Microwave energy is absorbed by liquids, so juices around food slow the cooking time. For foods to cook properly and for best flavor and nutrition, use very little water. You need only 1½ tablespoons of water for 5 cut-up carrots when using a dish with a lid. Frozen vegetables do not need any additional water at all because the frozen water crystals provide enough moisture. **With the microwave oven you can even adjust the moisture content and rejuvenate "stale" foods. This can be done by placing a small container of water in a corner of the microwave oven.** Use a cheese glass or shot glass with about ¾ inch of water in it. **The water will absorb some of the microwave energy but the steam from the water will "freshen" stale or dry foods.** The effect will be astonishing.

Density. Foods that are more dense cook more slowly than those that are less dense. For example, pork chops are more dense than meat loaf, and scalloped potatoes are more dense than mashed potatoes. Two pork chops take 3 to 4 minutes to reheat while two slices of meat loaf take 2 minutes. A cup of cold mashed potatoes takes 1 to 1½ minutes while a cup of scalloped potatoes takes 2 to 2½ minutes.

Quantity. The larger the amount of food you cook the more time required. For many foods doubling the quantity almost doubles the cooking time. For example, fresh breakfast rolls take 7 seconds for one, 15 seconds for two. When reheating food, as in a casserole, allow 30 to 45 seconds per serving.

AFTER-COOKING

Microwave energy causes the molecules within the food to move so rapidly against each other that they get very hot and thus cook the food from within. This method of cooking gives us very short cooking times but it also has another effect. This effect is that the molecules cannot immediately slow to their normal rate of movement after the cooking cycle is completed. This period of time is called after-cooking. The food will be at a serving temperature when the after-cooking is over.

Large dense foods such as roasts will continue to cook for about 15 to 20 minutes after being removed from the microwave oven. **All foods will stay hot for serving even longer than their after-cooking**

Continued on next page 19

time. For example, a 4-pound beef roast, which takes about 28 minutes for medium doneness, should sit for about 15 minutes before being carved. A 6-pound roast or a large turkey would be better after 20 minutes of after-cooking.

After-cooking will be quite obvious when you are cooking eggs. Stir scrambled eggs every 30 to 45 seconds, depending upon how many are being cooked, but be sure to take them out when they still look slightly damp. Fluff and serve them and they will be perfectly finished.

An egg should be poached for 45 seconds and then let sit in the water for 30 seconds or so outside the microwave oven before lifting it out with a slotted spoon.

Vegetables have almost no after-cooking. Squash and some of the more dense vegetables will stay hot much longer, but all others should be cooked at the last minute and served immediately.

ROTATING AND STIRRING

The pattern of the microwave energy within the oven leads to uneven cooking. The design of microwave ovens compensates for this unevenness by using stirrers and shelves. Although these are helpful, **it is still essential for you to allow for this uneven pattern by rotating the cooking container or stirring the food.** It is very easy to open the door to do this. The oven will shut itself off as soon as the door is opened. **This simple procedure of stirring will quickly become second nature to you.**

Different types of foods lend themselves to different methods for stirring or rotating. I will give a few general examples here, with more specific directions in the recipes.

Roasts. Turn large pieces of meat over and around every 10 minutes for 3 to 5 pound roasts and every 15 minutes for 5½ to 7 pound roasts when using High power.

Casseroles. A recipe that serves 4 to 6 people should have the container rotated every 3 minutes and will take 6 to 8 minutes to cook. **Stirring the casserole, if possible, works even better than rotating the container.** Whether a casserole can be stirred or not depends upon the type casserole that is being prepared. Large casseroles take longer to cook and if they cannot be stirred their edges will tend to dry a bit.

"Drying" Casseroles. To prevent a casserole from drying out, cut a half-inch strip of foil and put it just around the edge of the casserole, if the edges start to dry out. The microwave energy will bounce off the edge into the exposed food. Small amounts of foil (shielding) used in this way will not injure the magnetron tube.

Micro-cooking Power. In this book I have used only certain of the many power settings available on today's microwave ovens.

For power references the following table applies to the power settings that I have selected:

100% power—High power   30% power—Defrost, Low
 70% power—Roast, Medium High   10% power—Warm
 50% power—Simmer, Medium

COOKING *EN CONCERT*

Cooking **En Concert** means to enjoy your microwave oven to the fullest in partnership with the other cooking appliances in the kitchen. You will find that this concept will bring new dimensions to microwave cooking.

Beef Wellington, Canard à l'Orange, Stuffed Trout and Chocolate Soufflé are among the many epicurean delights that will tempt your palate and impress your guests. You will achieve the bon vivant's delight in half the time and yet have the best of both worlds.

You will learn how your microwave oven can be a tremendous partner when preparing Elegant Entrées and Glorious Desserts. Menu suggestions are also included for that special occasion.

For those of us who love to cook but have limited time, the microwave oven is the answer. Entertaining elegantly with ease in today's busy lifestyle requires help. You have it with the microwave oven. Enjoy!

Crab Fondue

Serves 4–6

1	**4 oz. jar Kraft Old English cheese spread**	**½**	**teaspoon Worcestershire sauce**
1	**8 oz. pkg. cream cheese**	**3**	**drops tabasco sauce**
1	**7 oz. can crab meat, undrained**		**dash garlic powder**

1) Place cream cheese in 2-quart measure. Soften on 70% power 1 minute.
2) Stir cream cheese with fork and add remaining ingredients except crab. Micro-cook on 70% power 4-6 minutes, stirring twice.
3) Stir in crab.

My cooking time _____

Hong Kong Style Canapes
Serves 10–12

2 lbs. chicken breasts, boned and cut into bite-size pieces	**½ teaspoon salt**
	½ teaspoon pepper
1 teaspoon curry powder	**2 tablespoons butter**
½ teaspoon Accent	

1) Mix curry powder, salt, pepper and Accent together and season chicken with mixture. Let stand for 30 minutes.
2) Melt butter in 10″ dish on High power 20-30 seconds.
3) Saute chicken in butter on High power 2-4 minutes. Stir twice.

Sauce

3 tablespoons chunk style peanut butter
3 tablespoons apple sauce

4) Combine peanut butter and apple sauce in a glass bowl.
5) Heat on High power 1-2 minutes. Serve as sauce into which chicken is dipped. Serve chicken on a plate with toothpicks.

My cooking time _____

Mushroom Canapes
Makes 3 dozen appetizers

3 cups large mushrooms, sliced (about 20 mushrooms, each 1½ inches in diameter)	**salt**
	36 pieces melba toast or toasted bread rounds
1 cup whipping cream	

1) Salt mushrooms to taste and place in a 7″ × 11″ glass baking dish. Cover with cream.
2) Micro-cook on High power 14-18 minutes until cream is very thick and has browned. Stir frequently.
3) Transfer mushrooms and cream to a chafing dish and keep hot.
4) Serve by spooning on toast.

My cooking time _____

Parmesan Fondue

Serves 8–10

2 8 oz. pkgs. cream cheese
1¾ to 2 cups milk
3 cloves (small) garlic,
   crushed
1 5 oz. pkg. fresh Parmesan
   cheese, grated

⅛ teaspoon salt
2 green onions, chopped
1 large loaf sourdough French
   bread, cut into 1" cubes
   freshly ground pepper

1) Place cream cheese in 1½-quart dish. Soften on 70% power 2 minutes.
2) Blend in milk to form a smooth sauce.
3) Micro-cook on 70% power 6-7 minutes, stirring frequently with fork or wire whisk. Add more milk, if needed, to obtain consistency for dipping.
4) Season with pepper. Stir.
5) Sprinkle onion on top and serve

Tip: This dish can be reheated several times.

My cooking time _____

Yummy Wingtips

Serves 6–8

1 lb. chicken wings
2 tablespoons Taco mix

4 tablespoons dry bread
   crumbs
   milk

1) Combine Taco mix and bread crumbs in medium size dish.
2) Dip wingtips in milk then into Taco-crumbs mixture.
3) Place wingtips in 8" round dish with meaty part of wingtips toward edge of dish (spoke-shaped). Cover with heavy plastic film for first 6 minutes.
4) Micro-cook on High power 12-14 minutes. Rotate dish once.
5) Allow to after-cook 5 minutes.

My cooking time _____

Ayam Goreng   Serves 4
DEEP-FAT FRIED CHICKEN WITH CHUTNEY AND RICE

2	chicken breasts, split (2 lbs. total)	2	teaspoons 5 Spice Powder (found where oriental foods are sold)
2	slices ginger root		
1	cup chicken broth	½	teaspoon tarragon

1) In a covered casserole dish, place the broth, ginger root, 5 Spice Powder and breasts. Poach on High power for 14-16 minutes.
2) Allow chicken to cool then remove skin.
3) *Dip chicken into batter and fry in cooking oil on conventional cooktop until brown.*
4) Drain on paper towels. Place on platter of cooked rice; serve with chutney.

Batter

½	cup flour	½	cup plus 2 tablespoons sherry
2	tablespoons wine vinegar		

5) Beat all ingredients together to make batter.

My cooking time _____

27

Chutney Chicken Roulade

Roulade

⅓ cup butter
½ cup flour
⅛ teaspoon salt
2 cups milk

4 eggs, separated
1 teaspoon sugar
  bread crumbs

1) Melt butter in a 4-cup measure on High power 45-60 seconds.
2) Gradually add flour and salt, stirring constantly. Micro-cook on High power 3-4 minutes until thick and smooth.
3) Slightly beat egg yolks. Add yolks and sugar to butter mixture, stirring constantly as they are added.
4) Beat egg whites until stiff. Stir in one-fourth of egg whites. Fold in remaining egg whites.
5) Grease a 10″ × 15″ jelly roll pan. Line pan with wax paper and grease paper. Spread roulade into pan.
6) *Bake in conventional oven at 300°F 30-40 minutes until golden.* Invert pan on waxed paper that has been sprinkled with bread crumbs. Remove pan and peel off paper. Set aside while making filling.

Tip: Roulade can be made ahead of time and frozen. Defrost overnight in refrigerator, then warm in microwave oven on 50% power 45-60 seconds before rolling out.

Chutney Chicken Filling
(Enough for Two Roulades)

6 tablespoons flour
6 tablespoons butter
1½ teaspoon curry powder
1½ cups hot chicken broth
  pinch of salt
⅛ teaspoon cayenne
1 tablespoon lemon juice

¾ cup lowfat yogurt
½ cup chutney, chopped fine
2 cups chicken breasts, cooked and shredded
  sour cream to garnish
  parsley to garnish

7) Melt butter in 4-cup measure on High power 1½ minutes.

8) Stir in curry powder, then gradually add flour, stirring constantly. Micro-cook on High power 1½ minutes until bubbly.

9) Slowly stir in chicken broth. Add salt and cayenne and micro-cook on High power 2-3 minutes more until thick. Stir two or three times.

10) Stir in lemon juice, yogurt, chutney and chicken. Micro-cook on 70% power 2 minutes more. Do not boil after yogurt has been added.

11) Roll out roulade. Spread filling to within one half inch of edge of roulade. Roll roulade up. Slice pieces 1-1½ inches thick. Garnish each slice with sour cream and parsley.

Tip: If it is necessary to reheat filling, use 70% power 1-2 minutes.

My cooking time _____

Herbed Chicken En Croute
Serves 6–8

1 uncooked 9″ pie crust (See ALL PURPOSE PIE CRUST recipe)

Chicken filling

2 cups chicken, cooked and cubed or shredded	½ cup fresh mushrooms, sliced thin
1 7 oz. can water chestnuts, sliced	1 tablespoon butter
1 cup canned or fresh Thompson seedless grapes	

1) Place butter in a 1-quart dish and melt on High power 15-20 seconds. Add mushrooms and micro-cook on High power 3-4 minutes until soft.

2) Add chicken, water chestnuts and grapes. Stir and set aside.

Continued on next page   29

Sauce

3	tablespoons butter	¼	teaspoon salt
3	tablespoons flour	⅛	teaspoon white pepper
1½	cups milk	¼	teaspoon allspice
1½	cups chicken bouillon	¼	teaspoon dry mustard
2	egg yolks, beaten	¼	cup sauterne wine
2	teaspoons lemon juice		

3) Place butter in a 4-cup glass measure and melt on High power 45-60 seconds.
4) Add flour, stirring constantly.
5) Slowly add milk and bouillon. Continue to stir to blend. Micro-cook on High power 4-6 minutes to boil. Allow sauce to boil 30 seconds.
6) Add a small amount of sauce to egg yolks, stirring constantly.
7) Return egg yolks (with small amount of sauce) into sauce and micro-cook on High power 45-60 seconds.
8) Using a wire whisk, blend in seasonings, lemon juice and wine.
9) Add sauce to chicken mixture. Blend thoroughly.
10) Place chicken and sauce in a 2-quart oven-proof dish.
11) Roll out pie crust and cover chicken dish with crust. Slit top of crust in several places.
12) Micro-cook on High power 4-6 minutes then *move dish to a conventional oven, pre-heated to 375°F, for 6-8 minutes until crust is golden.*

My cooking time _____

Coq Au Vin

Serves 6

4½	lbs. of select chicken pieces	½	clove garlic, crushed
¼	cup flour	1	bay leaf
⅛	teaspoon nutmeg	⅛	teaspoon dried thyme
½	teaspoon salt	½	cup mushrooms, sliced
¼	teaspoon pepper	2	strips bacon cooked and crumbled
¼	teaspoon paprika		
2	teaspoons butter	¾	cup burgundy wine
6	fresh green onions, sliced		

30

Homade Spaghetti Sauce
(Taste of Home 2008)
pg 70

✓1 Small onion chopped
¼ Green pepper chopped
1 cup water
✓½# beef
1 can Tomato sauce 8 oz
✓1 can diced tomatoes 8 oz
1 can tomato paste
2 Tbs minced parsley
✓2 gloves garlic minced
1 tsp italian season
✓ tsp Sugar   Salt
   pepper

1) Combine flour, nutmeg, salt, pepper and paprika in a paper bag. Shake individual chicken pieces in bag to coat.
2) *On conventional cooktop, melt butter in a 10" frying pan. Add green onions, garlic, bay leaf and thyme. Saute 1-2 minutes until onions are slightly limp.*
3) *Add chicken pieces and brown on all sides,* then place chicken pieces and butter mixture in a 10" casserole dish.
4) Add mushrooms and cover dish with lid. Micro-cook on High power 2-4 minutes.
5) Add bacon and wine. Stir to blend. Re-cover dish and micro-cook on 70% power 15-20 minutes until chicken is fork tender.
6) Allow to after-cook 10 minutes, covered.

My cooking time _____

Cornish Game Hens
With Chocolate-Orange Glaze
Serves 4

4 Cornish hens (room temperature)	1 tablespoon oil
	1 tablespoon instant cocoa
1 medium onion, quartered	⅛ teaspoon salt
⅓ cup Grand Marnier liqueur	parsley

1) Rinse hens thoroughly and pat dry with paper towels. Salt and pepper cavities. Place one-quarter onion in each hen.
2) In small container combine Grand Marnier, cocoa and oil. Pour 1 teaspoon of sauce into each hen cavity. Brush sauce over outside of hens.
3) Place hens, breast side down, on microwave roasting rack in a 9" × 13" dish. Micro-cook on High power 15 minutes.
4) Turn hens breast side up and brush with sauce. Micro-cook on High power 10-12 minutes more.
5) Brush hens again with sauce. Allow to after-cook 5 minutes.
6) Decorate around cavity openings with parsley.

My cooking time _____

En Concert Holiday Turkey

Serves 8–10

1	16 lb. turkey	½	cup fresh parsley, chopped
1	9½ oz. pkg. corn bread mix	2	teaspoons dried marjoram
½	cup raisins	1	teaspoon dried thyme
¼	cup rum	1	teaspoon salt
2	cups chopped onion	½	teaspoon pepper
2	cloves garlic, crushed	2	eggs, slightly beaten
½	cup butter	1	10 oz. pkg. baby carrots in
1½	cups tart apples, grated		butter
1	cup finely chopped celery	1	10 oz. pkg. Brussels sprouts
1	7½ oz. can water chestnuts,	½	lb. ground sausage
	drained and chopped fine		

Day Before

1) Place turkey in marinade sauce from BARBARA'S POTTED TURKEY recipe.

2) Make corn bread as directed on package. Micro-cook in 8" baking dish on High power 5-6 minutes. Rotate once. Allow to after-cook 5 minutes. Save for next day.

3) Soak raisins in rum overnight.

The Day

1) Remove turkey from marinade and let come to room temperature.

2) Melt butter in 10" casserole dish on High power 60-75 seconds.

3) Saute onion and garlic in butter on High power 3-4 minutes until tender. Stir twice.

4) Add sausage. Micro-cook on High power 3-4 minutes more. Sausage should lose its pinkness.

5) Stir in apples and celery. Micro-cook on High power 3-4 minutes more until apples and celery become soft. Drain.

6) Cut corn bread into one-half inch cubes. Combine corn bread, raisins, rum and sausage mixture. Blend well. Add eggs to mixture and toss mixture with fork.

7) Pat turkey dry with paper towel. Fill cavities loosely with sausage stuffing.

8) Place leftover stuffing in 2-quart dish with lid. Insert turkey neck in center of leftover stuffing for added flavor. Cover with plastic film, then lid. Place in refrigerator to cook later.

9) Place turkey, breast side down, on microwave roasting rack in a 9" × 13" dish. Micro-cook on High power 3½ minutes per pound. Turn turkey on its back after half the cooking time.

10) *Remove from microwave oven and roast in conventional oven preheated to 375°F. Roast for 20 minutes per pound or, if temperature probe is used, when thickest part of inside thigh reaches 170°F.*

11) Tent turkey with foil and allow to stand 20 minutes before carving.

12) While turkey is after-cooking, prepare carrots and Brussels sprouts. Puncture the box or pouch twice. Micro-cook on High power 6-8 minutes for carrots, 5-6 minutes for Brussels sprouts. Shake box or pouch once.

My cooking time _____

Beef Stroganoff

Serves 8

1½ lbs. top round steak, cut into strips 4" × 1" × ½"	¼ cup sour cream
2 tablespoons oil	2 teaspoons white vinegar
½ lb. fresh mushrooms, sliced thin	2 tablespoons water
1 10 oz. can cream of mushroom soup	1 clove garlic, crushed
	2 tablespoons fresh onion, finely minced
	2 teaspoons dry basil

1) *On conventional cooktop, saute meat in hot oil until lightly browned.*

2) Place meat into a 7½" × 11½" baking dish. Spread mushrooms over meat.

3) In the pan in which the meat was browned, combine the remaining ingredients in order to use the meat juices in the sauce. Pour the sauce over the meat and mushrooms.

4) Cover with heavy plastic film vented at one corner. Micro-cook on 50% power 15-18 minutes. Stir after 8 and 13 minutes. Stir from outside of dish toward the center. Replace plastic film during cooking, if necessary.

5) Allow to after-cook 10 minutes covered. Serve with rice.

My cooking time _____

The Potted Roast

2½	lb. chuck roast	1	package dry onion soup
¼	cup flour	¼	cup water
1	tablespoon instant cocoa	2	cups fresh mushrooms,
½	teaspoon salt		sliced
¼	teaspoon pepper	2	slices lemon
¼	cup oil	½	teaspoon fine herbs
½	cup burgundy wine	¼	teaspoon caraway seeds

1) Mix salt, pepper, cocoa and flour. Dredge meat in flour mixture.
2) *In a heavy skillet on conventional cooktop, brown roast in oil.* Drain off excess oil.
3) Add remaining ingredients to a 10″ baking dish with cover. Place meat in baking dish and cover.
4) Micro-cook on 30% power 30-45 minutes. Turn roast twice. Roast should be fork tender.
5) Allow to after-cook 10 minutes.

My cooking time _____

Barbecued, Marinated Roast Beef   Serves 10–12

1 6 lb. rolled, rib roast of beef

Marinade

1	cup red wine	1	clove garlic, quartered
1	medium onion, peeled and	2	bay leaves, crumbled
	chopped fine	½	teaspoon dried thyme leaves

Day before

1) Mix marinade ingredients in bowl (with lid) large enough to hold roast.
2) Pat roast with damp paper towels and prick meat with long-tined fork. Place roast in marinade and roll meat around. Refrigerate. Turn meat occasionally.

The day

Barbecue over a low fire 2½-3 hours or micro-cook on microwave roasting rack in baking dish on High power 7 minutes per pound for medium doneness. Turn roast over and around every 15 minutes.

My cooking time _____

Elegant Beef Wellington   Serves 6–8

1 4-lb. boneless, rolled sirloin tip roast	coarsely ground pepper
1 rib celery, chopped fine	¼ cup regular strength beef broth
1 onion, chopped fine	1 egg
½ lb. fresh mushrooms, chopped fine	2 tablespoons milk
1 tablespoon butter	2 10 oz. pkgs. frozen patty shells, defrosted

1) Tie string around roast to maintain its shape. Place roast, fat side down, on microwave roasting rack in a 2-quart utility dish. Cover with paper towel.
2) Micro-cook on High power 12 minutes. Turn meat over; drain off juices, reserving 2 tablespoons.
3) Rub roast with pepper. Place two tablespoons of drained juice in utility dish. Add celery and onion.
4) Return roast to rack. Micro-cook on High power 12 minutes more.
5) Remove roast from microwave oven and place on a separate dish. Allow to after-cook 15 minutes, then refrigerate until meat is cool to touch.
6) While roast is cooking, add beef broth, mushrooms and butter to vegetables. Stir. Micro-cook on High power 3-5 minutes until liquid is reduced to half original amount and vegetables are tender. Cover and set aside.
7) When meat is cool, remove cord and cut off excess fat.
8) On a bread board or cutting board, overlap patty shells in 3 rows of 4 shells each. Roll out pastry to a rectangle large enough to enclose the roast, about 12″ × 16″.

Continued on next page

9) Carefully place roast in center of dough. Drain any excess liquid from vegetables and use a slotted spoon to spread vegetables evenly over top and sides of roast.
10) Wrap pastry around roast, turning in the ends and pressing all seams together.

Tip: Moisten fingers with water to help seal seam as you press.

11) Place roast, seam side down, on conventional rimmed baking sheet. Make a small hole at each end of dough for steam to escape.
12) Decorate top with remaining pastry. Beat egg and milk with wire whisk and brush on entire crust.
13) *Place Beef Wellington in conventional oven preheated to 450°F. Immediately turn temperature down to 375°F. Bake 50-60 minutes until golden brown.* Let stand 15-20 minutes. Slice into ¾-inch slices and serve with Quick Brown Gravy.

Quick Brown Gravy

1 pkg. gravy mix	¼ cup roast drippings (fat skimmed off)
¼ cup red wine	½ cup water

14) Mix all ingredients in a 4-cup glass measure. Micro-cook on High power 3-5 minutes until thick.

My cooking time _____

En Concert Chateaubriand   Serves 6–8

2½ lbs. Chateaubriand	1 tablespoon brandy
4 oz. blue cheese	

1) Carefully trim fat from surface of meat. Make a slanting cut, 2 inches deep, the full length of the meat with a sharp knife held at a 45-degree angle. Make a similar cut on opposite side.

2) Blend cheese and brandy in a small container. (If necessary, soften cheese in microwave oven on High power 45 seconds then blend.)
3) Spread cheese mixture in the two cuts. Use short wooden skewers to close cuts. Tie string around ends and around middle of meat.
4) *Barbecue over hot coals 40 minutes, turning once after 20 minutes.*
5) Place meat on microwave roasting rack and micro-cook on 70% power 10-12 minutes. (If a micro-thermometer is used, set at 125°.)
6) Allow to after-cook 15 minutes. Untie, carve on a slant.

My cooking time _____

Gigot Romarin
LAMB WITH ROSEMARY

Serves 5–6

1	4-5 lb. leg of lamb	2	tablespoons cooking oil
	Dijon Prepared mustard (½	5	cloves garlic, sliced
	of a 4½ oz. jar)		salt and pepper to taste
	fresh or dried rosemary		

1) *On conventional cooktop, heat oil in a large skillet. Sear lamb on all sides in the hot oil.*
2) *Preheat conventional oven to 375°F.*
3) Remove lamb from skillet. Make a few slits on each side of lamb and insert sliced garlic cloves. Smear lamb with mustard and press the rosemary onto the lamb.
4) *Place lamb on roasting rack and roast in oven for 30 minutes.*
5) Season with salt and pepper and place on microwave oven roasting rack in a 7½" × 11½" baking dish. Micro-cook on High power 18-20 minutes. Turn lamb over and around twice.
6) Tent with foil and allow to after-cook 20 minutes. Serve with mint jelly.

My cooking time _____

Gingersnap Sauerbraten

4 lb. rump roast
1 cup red wine vinegar
1 cup water
2 tablespoons granulated sugar
2 tablespoons instant cocoa
2 bay leaves
1 teaspoon garlic salt

½ teaspoon pepper
1 medium onion, sliced
3 tablespoons oil
½ cup gingersnap crumbs (10 cookies)
¼ cup raisins
2 tablespoons brown sugar

Marinate roast 2 to 4 days ahead of time by:

1) In a 4-cup measure combine vinegar, water, granulated sugar, cocoa, bay leaves, garlic salt and pepper. Micro-cook to boiling on High power 3-5 minutes.
2) Place roast in 2-quart container. Pour marinade and onion over roast. Cover and refrigerate 2-4 days.

To cook roast:

3) *In a heavy skillet on conventional cooktop, brown roast in oil.*
4) Place roast in 3-quart casserole dish, cover lightly with plastic film, or cover with lid.
5) Micro-cook on 30% power 50-65 minutes until fork tender. Turn roast twice.
6) Remove from microwave oven. Place roast on a large dish and cover with foil. Allow to after-cook 15 minutes.
7) While roast is after-cooking, add gingersnap crumbs, raisins, brown sugar and remaining marinade to casserole dish. Micro-cook on High power 5-6 minutes. Stir.
8) After roast has after-cooked, cut into ¼" thick slices. Add slices to marinade and micro-cook on 50% power 2-3 minutes. Stir.

My cooking time _____

Canard à l'Orange

1	4-5 lb. duck, completely defrosted and at room temperature	1	apple, cored and quartered
		1	orange, peeled very thin and seeded (reserve peel)
1	rib celery		white pepper

Sauce (Enough for two ducks)

¼	cup granulated sugar	⅓	cup dry sherry
2	tablespoons red wine vinegar	3	drops tabasco sauce
		3	drops orange extract
1½	cups chicken broth	3	tablespoons cornstarch
2	tablespoons currant jelly		white pepper
1	cup fresh orange juice		salt and pepper
¼	cup tap water		

Preparing the duck.

1) Rinse thawed duck under tap water after removing giblets.
2) Pat duck dry with paper towel, then prick all over with a long-tined fork.
3) Rub liberally with white pepper. Stuff with celery, apple and orange.
4) Tie legs together with string. Place breast side down on a microwave roasting rack in a 2-quart utility dish. Cover with a paper towel.
5) Micro-cook on High power 20 minutes. Rotate dish after 10 minutes.
6) Drain off juices. Place duck, breast up, on the rack and micro-cook 20 minutes more on High power. Rotate dish after 10 minutes.
7) Test for doneness in ease of movement of duck legs. Remove from microwave oven, cover with foil and allow to after-cook while preparing the sauce.

Sauce

8) Cut orange peel in fine julienne strips. Place in small mixing bowl and cover with boiling water. Let stand a few minutes, drain and set aside.

Continued on next page   39

9) *In a microwave usable dish, caramelize sugar on conventional cooktop, stirring constantly until sugar melts and is golden in color.*
10) Add wine vinegar carefully, stirring constantly.
11) Add orange juice, currant jelly, orange peel and chicken broth.
12) Micro-cook on High power 10 minutes. Stir 3 times.
13) Add sherry, tabasco and orange extract. Salt and pepper to taste. Micro-cook on High power 2 minutes more.
14) Combine cornstarch and water. Stir to a smooth paste.
15) Add cornstarch mixture to sauce, stirring constantly.
16) Micro-cook on High power 3-4 minutes until sauce thickens and boils. Allow sauce to after-cook 5 minutes.
17) Arrange serving platter with parsley and orange slices with a small amount of currant jelly in center of slices.
18) Place duck on platter and pour one-fourth of sauce over duck. Serve remaining sauce in a pitcher.

Tip: Sauce can be made in advance and stored in refrigerator 2-3 days.
When cooking two ducks, it is best to cook one at a time. Duck(s) can be reheated from room temperature on High power in 2-3 minutes.

My cooking time _____

Chili Crepes

14–16 crepes

Crepes

1 cup pancake mix	2 eggs
1 tablespoon cornmeal	1 tablespoon cooking oil
1 cup milk	¼ teaspoon onion salt

1) Blend all ingredients together in blender or food processor. Refrigerate for 2 hours.
2) *Make crepes in electric crepe-maker or a frying pan. Can be made ahead of time.*

Filling

1 pkg. Taco seasoning mix	1 cup Cheddar cheese, grated
1 16 oz. can chili beans	sour cream and parsley
1 lb. ground beef	

3) Mix one half of Taco mix with ground beef in a 2-quart measure. Micro-cook on High power 3 minutes. Stir once.
4) Add beans and micro-cook on High power 3 minutes more. Stir and micro-cook on High power 1 minute more.

To Assemble

5) Lay out crepes.
6) Sprinkle each crepe with cheese, then spoon beef mixture onto each crepe.
7) Roll each crepe and place them seam side down in a 9″ × 13″ baking dish. Sprinkle remaining Taco mix over crepes.
8) Micro-cook on 70% power 4-5 minutes.
9) Cover with plastic film and allow to after-cook 5 minutes. Garnish with sour cream and parsley.

My cooking time _____

Sumptuous Artichokes With Seafood

Serves 6–8

8 large artichokes, trimmed and rubbed with lemon juice	1½ cup croutons
	1 teaspoon dry tarragon
¼ cup butter	½ teaspoon dried dill
8 green onions, chopped	½ teaspoon celery seed
2 cloves garlic, minced	½ teaspoon paprika
¾ lb. mushrooms, sliced	¼ cup dry sherry
2 lbs. (total) scallops or shrimp or combination, cut into bite-size pieces	1½ cup Hollandaise sauce (See HOLLANDAISE SAUCE II recipe)

1) Place 4 artichokes at a time in a 10″ baking dish with a lid. Micro-cook each set of 4 artichokes on High power 12-15 minutes. Set aside, covered.

Continued on next page 41

2) Melt butter in 10" dish on High power 45-60 seconds. Saute onions, garlic and mushrooms in butter on High power 2-3 minutes.
3) Add seafood, croutons, tarragon, dill, celery seeds and paprika. Micro-cook on High power 4-5 minutes until seafood is just cooked.
4) Add sherry and micro-cook on High power 30 seconds more. Season with salt and pepper. Stir in one-half cup of Hollandaise sauce.
5) Spread artichoke leaves apart and fill space between leaves with seafood mixture. Top artichokes with remaining Hollandaise sauce. *Place under conventional broiler until top of sauce is lightly browned.*

Tip: Artichokes can be cooked and filled with seafood in advance. Refrigerate. Re-heat on 70% power 2-3 minutes.

My cooking time _____

Stuffed Trout

Serves 6-8

1 lb. salmon or sole, filleted and skinned	10 7-8 oz. trout, filleted but body "intact"
1 egg white	1½ cups fresh mushrooms, julienne
1 cup heavy cream	
½ teaspoon salt	1½ cups fresh carrots, julienne
¼ teaspoon ground white pepper	1½ cups zucchini, julienne
½ teaspoon dry tarragon	1 cup dry white wine
2 tablespoons parsley, chopped	¼ cup butter
	salt and pepper to taste
1 tablespoon fresh or dried chives	

Stuffing (Can be made a day ahead)

1) Cut salmon or sole into small pieces and puree in food processor or blender. Add egg white and continue blending a little at a time until puree is smooth.

2) While processor or blender is still running, *slowly* add heavy cream, salt, white pepper, tarragon and parsley. Blend well. Place in a bowl and refrigerate, covered.

Trout

3) Rinse gutted and boned fish thoroughly. Pat dry with paper towel. Set fish aside.
4) Lightly butter a 9" × 13" baking dish and a 7½" × 11½" dish. Sprinkle each dish with half the vegetable mixture. Set the dishes aside.
5) Cut a 6" × 6" square of wax paper for each trout.
6) Stuff each trout with about one-fourth cup of stuffing. Wrap each trout in a square of wax paper. Arrange fish in the two dishes on top of vegetables, alternating head to tail. Cover trout with remaining vegetables.
7) Pour ⅔ cup white wine into 9" × 13" dish and ⅓ cup wine into other dish.
8) Cover each dish with plastic film and micro-cook separately on High power 10-12 minutes for the 9" × 13" dish, then 8-10 minutes for the second dish. Rotate each dish half way through its cooking time. When done, fish should be opaque and should flake when pierced with a fork.
9) Remove trout from each cooking dish, skin if desired, and arrange on a large platter. Use a slotted spoon to place vegetables over the trout.
10) While second dish is micro-cooking, cover first dish with foil and *place in preheated conventional oven at 180°F.*
11) Repeat steps 10 and 11 for second dish.

Sauce

2	tablespoons butter	1 cup heavy cream
2	tablespoons flour	Poaching liquid remaining in
1	cube bouillon	2 cooking dishes

12) Place butter in a 4-cup measure and melt on High power 20-30 seconds. Slowly stir in flour until smooth.
13) Pour all the poaching liquid remaining from cooking the trout into the 7½" × 11½" dish and micro-cook on High power 4-6 minutes until liquid boils.

Continued on next page   43

14) Pour the hot liquid into the flour-butter mixture, stirring constantly. Blend well.
15) Bring liquid to a boil again on High power. Add bouillon cube and stir. Micro-cook on High power 1 minute more.
16) Stir liquid, add heavy cream and stir again. Micro-cook on 70% power 3 minutes more. Stir once or twice.
17) At this time, add any liquid that has accumulated on the fish platter to the sauce. Blend. Salt and pepper to taste. Spoon sauce over fish and vegetables. Garnish with parsley.
18) Serve remaining sauce in a pitcher.

My cooking time _____

Dolmas
Serves 12

STUFFED GRAPE LEAVES

40 grape leaves (1 large jar)	3 tablespoons goat or Swiss cheese, grated
6 oz. ground veal	
6 oz. ground lamb	⅔ cup rice, cooked
6 oz. ground lean beef	¼ teaspoon salt
2 medium onions	⅛ teaspoon pepper
6 mint leaves	2 carrots, sliced
½ teaspoon dill weed	1 onion, sliced
	2 cups bouillon

1) Use a food processor to grind veal, lamb and ground beef. Set meats aside. Chop mint leaves and onions together in processor and set aside. Grate cheese in the processor. Combine the meats, mint and onion and cheese in a mixing bowl.
2) Rinse grape leaves well and drain in a colander.
3) Lay out a few grape leaves at a time and fill each one with 1 tablespoon of meat mixture rolled into a short cigar shape. Fold each leaf toward middle and roll, completely enclosing filling.
4) Place carrots and onion in a 2-quart dish with lid and micro-cook on High power 6 minutes. Set aside.
5) Arrange grape leaves in a lightly buttered 9″ × 13″ dish, folded side down. Leave a slight space between each leaf. Place

partially cooked carrots and onions on top, evenly. Pour bouillon over all.

6) Cover with plastic film vented at one corner. Micro-cook on 70% power 15-20 minutes. Remove from microwave oven and arrange on platter. Cover with foil to keep warm while preparing sauce.

Sauce

¼	cup butter	1½	cups chicken broth
5	tablespoons flour	1	egg yolk, beaten
⅛	teaspoon salt	1	teaspoon lemon juice
⅛	teaspoon pepper		

7) Place butter in a 4-cup measure and melt on High power 45-60 seconds. Stir in flour, salt and pepper, blending well. Slowly add broth to mixture and micro-cook on High power 4 minutes. Stir twice.

8) Beat egg yolk and lemon juice with a wire whisk several seconds to obtain volume. Add to broth mixture. Stir well. Micro-cook on 70% power 3-4 minutes until sauce thickens. Stir every 60 seconds. Remove container from microwave oven and cover with plastic film to keep warm.

To Serve

9) Arrange dolmas on a large serving platter, leaving center of platter empty. Cluster carrots and onions in center of platter. Pour sauce over grape leaves. Serve any remaining sauce with meal.

My cooking time _____

Apricot Cheese Cake

Serves 8–10

Crust

1   cup vanilla wafer crumbs   ¼   cup butter or margarine
2   tablespoons sugar

1) Melt butter in a 10″ round dish on High power 45-60 seconds.
2) Stir sugar and wafer crumbs into butter and press mixture evenly
   into bottom of dish.
3) Micro-cook on High power 2-3 minutes. Set aside to cool.

Filling

1   1 lb. can apricot halves   2   cups cottage cheese, pureed
1   12 oz. can apricot nectar   ⅓   cup sugar
2   envelopes unflavored gelatin   1   cup sour cream
3   eggs, separated   1   tablespoon lemon juice
1   8 oz. pkg. cream cheese,   1   tablespoon cornstarch
    softened

4) Drain apricot halves. Reserve juice.
5) Select 6-8 apricot halves to decorate top of cake. Set these
   aside.
6) Puree remaining apricot halves in food processor or blender.

7) Soften gelatin in ½ cup apricot nectar. Beat egg yolks and add them to gelatin mixture. Micro-cook on High power 2-3 minutes. Stir with wire whisk every 45 seconds.

8) Stir in pureed apricots and remaining apricot nectar. Allow to cool until partially set.

9) Combine cream cheese, cottage cheese, sour cream, sugar and lemon juice in a small container. Blend into apricot-gelatin mixture.

10) Beat egg whites until stiff peaks form. Fold whites into apricot-cheese mixture. Pour into cool crust and refrigerate 3 hours.

Top Glaze

11) Slice reserved apricot halves and arrange on cake.

12) Blend ¼ cup apricot juice with cornstarch.

13) Micro-cook remaining apricot juice on High power 3-5 minutes to reduce it to ½ cup.

14) Add cornstarch mixture to reduced apricot juice and micro-cook on High power 1-2 minutes until thick and clear. Stir frequently.

15) Allow to cool in refrigerator 10 minutes. Spoon liquid over cake and refrigerate cake for 30 minutes.

Tip: Use the most beautiful dish you have. A crystal one is most effective.

My cooking time _____

Holiday Rum Cake

Serves 12

1 cup chopped pecans or walnuts	4 eggs
1 (18½ oz.) pkg. yellow cake mix	½ cup cold water
1 (3½ oz.) pkg. Instant vanilla pudding	½ cup vegetable oil
	½ cup dark rum

Continued on next page 47

1) Grease a 3-quart bundt cake dish. (Grease generously if dish is ceramic, lightly if plastic.) Line bottom of dish with nuts. Set dish aside.
2) Combine cake mix, pudding mix, eggs, water, oil and rum in a large mixing bowl. Beat with electric mixer 4 minutes.
3) Pour 2 cups of batter gently over nuts, then add remaining batter.
4) Micro-cook on High power 10-12 minutes until a toothpick comes out clean. Rotate 3 times.
5) Allow cake to after-cook 10 minutes. Invert onto serving dish and glaze.

Glaze

½ cup butter or margarine	¼ cup water
1 cup granulated sugar	¼ cup dark rum

6) Place butter in 1-quart bowl and melt on High power 60-90 seconds.
7) Stir in sugar and water. Micro-cook on High power 2-3 minutes or until mixture boils. Stir in rum.
8) Prick top and sides of cake with fork tines. Dribble half of glaze evenly over cake. Allow cake to absorb glaze and repeat. (Save any unused glaze to serve on side or use for next cake.)
9) Garnish with maraschino cherries and whipped cream or—soak a sugar cube in lemon extract or brandy, place on top of cake and light with match.

My cooking time _____

Apple Pie

Serves 6 –8

1 Unbaked 9″ pie crust (See ALL PURPOSE PIE CRUST recipe)

5 tart green apples, peeled and sliced thin	1 tablespoon flour
	1 teaspoon cinnamon
1 cup sugar	1½ tablespoon butter or
1 tablespoon lemon juice	margarine
1 pint water	1 teaspoon milk

1) Mix lemon juice and water.
2) Place sliced apples into a bowl and cover with lemon-water mixture. Use enough lemon-water to keep apple slices covered.
3) Roll out one half of pie crust to fit 9″ pie plate. (Roll crust using a pastry cloth or between two pieces of wax paper.)
4) Place pie crust in pie plate and sprinkle with 1 teaspoon sugar.
5) Drain apples and combine them with flour, cinnamon and sugar.
6) Place mixture into pie shell. Do not mound mixture too high in center of shell.
7) Dot apple mixture with butter.
8) Roll out remainder of pie crust and place on top of apple mixture. Flute edges of crust and cut slits in top of crust.
9) Brush crust with milk and sprinkle with a little sugar. The sugar will cause crust to brown beautifully.
10) *Preheat conventional oven to 450°F.*
11) Micro-cook pie on High power 10-12 minutes until bubbles begin to show under the slits in crust. Rotate 3 times.
12) *Bake in conventional oven 15 minutes more until golden.*

My cooking time _____

Apricot Chiffon Pie

Serves 6–8

1 pre-baked 9″ pie crust (See ALL PURPOSE PIE CRUST recipe)

⅔	cup dried apricots	1	tablespoon lemon juice
½	cup sugar and ¼ cup sugar (measured separately)	3	egg whites
		1	cup water

1) Combine apricots and water in medium size bowl. Micro-cook on High power 6-7 minutes until fruit is soft. Stir and mash apricots every 2 minutes.
2) When apricots are soft, force them through strainer or use food processor to puree.
3) Combine apricot puree, ½ cup sugar and lemon juice.
4) Beat egg whites until foamy, adding ¼ cup sugar gradually. Continue beating whites to a stiff, shiny meringue.

Continued on next page   49

5) Fold apricot mixture into meringue and fill the pie shell with the filling.
6) *Bake in conventional oven at 375°F until delicately browned (3-5 minutes).* Serve warm or cold.

My cooking time _____

En Concert Oregon Blackberry Pie Serves 6–8

Use ALL PURPOSE PIE CRUST recipe. Make 2 crusts but do not bake them.

¾ **cup sugar**	3½ **cups blackberries**
3 **tablespoons cornstarch**	2 **teaspoons sugar**
½ **teaspoon cinnamon**	1 **tablespoon butter**
½ **cup blackberry juice**	1 **teaspoon milk**

1) If blackberries are frozen, make two holes in top of pouch or box with a fork. Place pouch on paper plate and heat on High power 4½ minutes. Let stand for 2 minutes, stir. If necessary, heat on High power 1-2 minutes more.
2) Blend dry ingredients (except the 2 teaspoons of sugar) in a 2-quart bowl. Gradually stir in blackberry juice.
3) Micro-cook on High power 2-3 minutes until mixture boils. Stir once or twice while cooking.
4) Arrange bottom pie crust in a pie plate and sprinkle 1 teaspoon of sugar over the crust.
5) Place blackberries in a bowl and pour hot liquid over berries. Mix gently.
6) Pour blackberry mixture carefully into pie shell. Dot with butter. Cover with second pie crust.
7) Make slits in top crust. Sprinkle top crust with last teaspoon of milk and then sugar. Micro-cook on High power 8-10 minutes until juice bubbles underneath the slits. Turn dish one-fourth turn 3 times while cooking.
8) *Remove and place in a conventional oven preheated to 425°F. Bake pie in oven 10-12 minutes until crust is golden.*

My cooking time _____

Black Bottom Pie

Serves 6–8

Gingersnap Pie Crust

24 gingersnaps
4 tablespoons butter

1) Use food processor or blender to make gingersnaps into fine crumbs.
2) Melt butter in a 9″ glass pie plate on High power 45-60 seconds. Mix gingersnap crumbs with butter and spread evenly over pie plate.
3) Micro-cook on High power 2-2½ minutes. Turn plate one fourth turn twice while cooking. Set aside.

Black Bottom Filling

½	tablespoon unflavored gelatin	4	egg yolks, beaten
2	tablespoons cold water	4	tablespoons light rum
1¾	cups milk	1	teaspoon vanilla
½	cup sugar	3	oz. semi-sweet chocolate,
2	tablespoons cornstarch		melted
¼	teaspoon salt		

1) Soften gelatin in water.
2) Place milk in 4-cup measure and scald on High power 1½-2 minutes.
3) Mix sugar, cornstarch and salt together. Stir slowly into milk. Micro-cook on High power 3-5 minutes until thick. Stir after 1 minute.
4) Gradually add egg yolks. Micro-cook on High power 1 minute more. Stir after 30 seconds.
5) Stir in rum and vanilla.
6) Melt chocolate in a small dish on High power 60-90 seconds. Stir often.
7) Add melted chocolate to 1 cup of custard to make the chocolate layer. Pour carefully into gingersnap crust. Chill for 30 minutes.
8) Stir gelatin into remaining custard and micro-heat on High power 1 minute to dissolve gelatin. Stir and let cool.

Continued on next page 51

Cream Layer

4 egg whites   **½ cup sugar**
⅛ teaspoon cream of tartar

1) Beat egg whites until frothy. Add cream of tartar. Continue beating, while adding sugar slowly, until whites form soft peaks.
2) Fold into cooled custard. Pour carefully over chocolate layer. Chill until custard is set. Garnish with chocolate curls.

My cooking time _____

Lemon Angel Pie

Serves 6–8

Meringue Shell

3 egg whites   **½ teaspoon cream of tartar**
1 cup sugar

1) Beat egg whites until foamy. Gradually add sugar mixed with cream of tartar until thoroughly blended. Beat until stiff but not dry.
2) Generously oil a 9″ pie plate being careful not to oil top edge.
3) Spread meringue in pie plate, building up sides slightly. *Bake in conventional oven at 275°F 1 hour. Turn off oven and let cool for several hours in oven (overnight is fine).*

Filling

3   egg yolks   **1   teaspoon lemon rind, grated**
1   whole egg   **2-3 tablespoons lemon juice**
½ cup sugar   **½ pint whipping cream**

4) Slightly beat egg yolks and whole egg together and put them in a 4-cup glass measure with sugar, lemon rind and lemon juice.
5) Micro-cook on High power 3-4 minutes until thick. Stir several times.

52

6) Whip the cream and fold into egg mixture.
7) Pour into meringue shell. Refrigerate. Garnish with orange peel.

My cooking time _____

Lemon Meringue Pie   Serves 6–8

1 pre-baked 9″ pie crust (See ALL PURPOSE PIE CRUST recipe)

Filling

1½ cup sugar	¼ cup lemon juice
⅓ cup cornstarch	1 tablespoon grated lemon
1½ cups water	peel
3 egg yolks, slightly beaten	½ teaspoon lemon extract
3 tablespoons butter	

1) Mix sugar, cornstarch and water in large mixing bowl. Micro-cook on High power 4-6 minutes until mixture thickens and boils. Stir every minute.
2) Pour small amount of hot mixture into egg yolks. Stir yolks while pouring in mixture.
3) Pour egg yolk mixture back into bowl containing hot mixture. Mix thoroughly.
4) Micro-cook mixture on High power 45-60 seconds. Stir well.
5) Add butter, lemon juice, lemon peel and lemon extract. Blend thoroughly. Pour into pie shell.

Meringue

3 egg whites	6 tablespoons sugar
¼ teaspoon cream of tartar	1 tablespoon toasted almonds

6) Beat cream of tartar into egg whites until frothy.
7) Gradually beat sugar into mixture, 2 tablespoons at a time.
8) Beat egg white mixture until it forms stiff peaks when beaters are raised.

Continued on next page   53

Tip: Meringue should feel like satin between the fingers—no granules.)

9) Carefully spread meringue onto lemon filling in pie shell. Spread meringue to sides of pie shell to seal the edge.
10) Sprinkle meringue with toasted, slivered almonds. Micro-cook on High power 2-4 minutes. Rotate dish several times. Micro-cook until a toothpick comes out clean.

My cooking time _____

Caramel Custard

Serves 4–6

This recipe requires a 1½ quart dish or 6 six to eight ounce individual dishes.

Caramel Sauce

¾ cup sugar

Melt sugar in a sauce pan or small skillet on conventional cooktop. Stir constantly. Heat until sugar is clear and just golden in color. Pour small amount into each individual dish (or all into large dish) coating the bottom. Let stand until caramel hardens.

Custard

3	eggs	2	cups milk
⅓	cup sugar	1	teaspoon vanilla extract
¼	teaspoon salt		

1) Place milk into 4-cup measure. Scald on high power 2½-3 minutes.
2) While milk is heating, beat eggs slightly and stir sugar in gradually. Blend well.
3) Stir milk and vanilla extract into egg-sugar mixture. Pour mixture into dishes or large dish.

4) Micro-cook on 50% power 10-12 minutes, rotating each dish twice. Cook until custard is barely set. Allow custard to after-cook 15 minutes. After-cooking will make the custard firm.
5) Unmold onto serving dish. Caramel sauce will glaze the custard. Serve at room temperature or chilled.

My cooking time _____

Cherries Jubilee Flambé

Serves 6–8

1 tablespoon cornstarch	1 cup warm brandy
1 tablespoon sugar	dash of lemon juice
1 can (1 lb.) pitted Bing cherries, including liquid	scoops of French vanilla ice cream
3 or 4 strips orange peel	

1) Mix cornstarch and sugar in medium size bowl.
2) Gradually stir in cherry liquid and orange peel.
3) Micro-cook on High power 3 minutes or until thick. Stir once.
4) Add cherries and lemon juice. Mix thoroughly.
5) At the table, gently ladle brandy over top of sauce. Ignite using a long match. (Have lights turned down.)
6) Spoon over ice cream while sauce is still flaming.

My cooking time _____

Chocolate Soufflé

Serves 6–8

1 teaspoon instant coffee	1 teaspoon vanilla extract
¼ cup water	4 egg yolks
1¼ cups half and half	6 egg whites
6 oz. semi-sweet chocolate chips	4 tablespoons sugar
3 tablespoons butter	¼ teaspoon salt
3 tablespoons flour	¼ teaspoon cream of tartar

Continued on next page   55

1) Lightly butter 2-quart soufflé dish and dust with sugar.
2) Bring water to boil in microwave oven then add instant coffee. Stir to dissolve.
3) In a large glass measuring cup combine half and half, chocolate chips and coffee.
4) Micro-cook on 70% power 5 minutes, stirring once. After 5 minutes, stir until all chocolate dissolves.
5) While chocolate-coffee liquid is cooking, *melt butter in 2-quart saucepan on conventional cooktop.*
6) *Add flour to butter and stir until bubbly.*
7) *Gradually add chocolate-coffee liquid to butter, stirring constantly. (Stir with wire whisk.)*
8) *Continue cooking mixture on cooktop until it thickens (3-4 minutes). Add vanilla extract and stir.*
9) While mixture is cooking on cooktop, beat egg yolks with 3 tablespoons sugar until light. (Reserve 1 tablespoon sugar for egg whites.)
10) Add a little chocolate mixture to yolks and blend well, then pour this back into saucepan with remaining chocolate mixture and blend thoroughly.
11) *Place over low heat on cooktop for 1 minute, stirring constantly.* Transfer to 3-4 quart bowl and let cool a few minutes.
12) In a separate bowl, beat egg whites until foamy. Add salt and cream of tartar and beat until soft peaks form.
13) Add remaining sugar (1 tablespoon) and continue beating until stiff but not dry.
14) Fold a large spoonful of whites into chocolate mixture, then carefully fold in remaining whites.
15) Gently spoon into prepared soufflé dish. Micro-cook on 30% power 17-19 minutes. Rotate dish one-fourth turn every 4 minutes.
16) Serve immediately. Scoop from center of soufflé into individual serving dishes.
17) Garnish with powdered sugar. May be served with whipped cream or vanilla ice cream.

My cooking time _____

Raspberry Chantilly

Serves 6

1	10 oz. pkg. frozen raspberries	½	cup whipping cream
1	tablespoon cornstarch	4	teaspoons sugar
	pinch of salt	½	cup sour cream
		½	teaspoon vanilla

1) Puncture raspberry package with a fork and defrost on High power 2 minutes. Drain and reserve syrup.
2) In a 4-quart measure mix cornstarch, salt and syrup. Micro-cook on High power 2-3 minutes until thick and clear. Stir twice. Set aside to cool.
3) Combine whipping cream and sugar and beat until stiff. Fold in sour cream and vanilla.
4) In parfait glasses or large wine glasses, layer cream mixture and raspberries. Chill.

My cooking time _____

Menus for Entertaining

*Coq au Vin
Endive salad
French baguette and sweet butter
*Raspberry Chantilly

*Stuffed Trout
*Concombres cuits (cucumbers)
Popovers with sweet butter
*Tomatoes Vinaigrette
Fruit Ice
*Spicy Pumpkin Squares

*Canard à l'Orange
Wild rice
*Fresh asparagus
Parker House rolls
*Chocolate Soufflé

*En Concert Holiday Turkey
*Cranberry sauce
*Best white onions
*Braised parsnips with Brussels sprouts
Cranberry Waldorf salad
*Holiday Rum Cake

*Beef Wellington
*Scalloped potatoes
*Broccoli with Hollandaise sauce
Strawberry Pineapple jello
Cloverleaf rolls
*Caramel custard

*Dolmas(Stuffed grape leaves)
Tabbouleh salad
Armenian bread
*Black Bottom pie

*Recipe is in this book.

Continued on next page

*Gingersnap Sauerbraten
Mit spatzle (small noodles)
Sweet and sour red cabbage
Fresh fruit salad
*Apple pie

*The Potted Roast
*Parslied potatoes
*Carrots and Currants
Tomato aspic
Butterfly rolls
*Chocolate Pudding cake

*Herbed Chicken en Croute
Orange jello cabbage slaw
French rolls
Petite green peas
*Apricot Cheesecake

*En Concert Chateaubriand
Jellied beet salad
*Baked potato with chives
French bread
*Blackberry pie

*Beef Stroganoff
Poppy seed noodles
*Green beans with toasted almonds
Orange grapefruit jello mold
*Apricot Chiffon pie

*Chutney Chicken Roulade
with raisins and peanuts
Tossed green salad with
Mandarin oranges and red onion
French rolls
*Poached pears with raspberry sauce

*Recipe is in this book.

*Barbecued, Marinated Roast Beef
Twice baked potatoes
Spinach salad
*Pound cake with fresh fruit

*Ayam Goreng (Deep-fat fried chicken)
with chutney
Rice
*Green Beans Spécial
Tossed salad
*Lemon Meringue pie

*Gigot Romarin (Lamb with rosemary)
Barley pilaf
*Red Cabbage
Lettuce salad with lemon dressing
*Cherries Jubilee Flambe

*Artichoke and Seafood
Crusty bread
*Lemon Angel pie

*Chili Crepes
Avocado-tomato salad or
Shredded lettuce
Fruit Ice and cookies

*Cornish Game Hen with
Chocolate-orange glaze
Wild rice
*Artichokes
24 Hour salad
*Chocolate Potato cake

*Recipe is in this book.

THE MAID IS IN

Your microwave oven is literally the "maid" in the kitchen when it comes to saving time in cooking and heating food. Equally rewarding, is the fact that cleanup time in the kitchen is reduced 50%.

Here you will find dozens of delicious recipes, some using only the microwave oven, others micro-cooked *en concert*. All are delectable, nutritious and eye-appealing.

Follow this easy code to help you decide which recipe will fit into your schedule for the day. After-cooking time is included. *Don't forget though, micro-cooking times are all rapid in comparison to conventional cooking times:*

 — Indicates a cooking time of 15 minutes or less.

 — Indicates a cooking time of 16-30 minutes.

 — Indicates a cooking time of more than 30 minutes.

NOTE: Individual preparation time is not included.

Now, cook in your microwave oven and enjoy your Maid in the Kitchen.

Chicken Divan

Serves 6

3½ lbs. of chicken breasts
2 10 oz. pkgs. frozen broccoli spears

½ cup sharp cheese, shredded
celery salt
onion salt

1) Cut breasts in half and arrange in a 2-quart dish with meat side toward edge of dish.
2) Sprinkle with celery and onion salts. Cover with heavy plastic film.
3) Micro-cook on High power 12-14 minutes until chicken is fork tender.
4) Chill breasts for ease in slicing. Skin, bone and slice breast meat into thick slices.
5) Punch two or more holes in broccoli package or pouch. Micro-cook right in package on High power 8-10 minutes. Shake package twice while cooking.

Sauce

1 10½ oz. can cream of chicken soup
½ cup mayonnaise

¼ cup milk
1 teaspoon lemon juice
½ teaspoon curry powder

Mix all ingredients in a small bowl and set aside.

Bread Crumb Mix

½ cup soft bread crumbs   pimiento
1 tablespoon butter

6) Place butter and bread crumbs in a custard cup and micro-cook on High power 25-35 seconds. Stir.
7) Arrange broccoli in 7½" × 11½" glass dish with flowers toward edge of dish (alternate broccoli spears). Place sliced chicken over broccoli stalks.
8) Pour sauce over chicken. Sprinkle cheese on top, then sprinkle bread crumb mixture over all. Garnish with pimiento or toasted almonds. Cover with heavy plastic film.
9) Micro-cook on High power 6-8 minutes. Rotate dish once.

Tip: This dish can be made ahead of time and refrigerated. If refrigerated, heat on High power 8-10 minutes before serving. Rotate dish once while heating.

My cooking time _____

Poulet Aux Artichauts
CHICKEN WITH ARTICHOKES

Serves 8

2 pkgs. frozen artichoke hearts
3 cups chicken, diced
1 10½ oz. can cream of chicken soup
1 cup mayonnaise
½ cup milk or half and half
1 teaspoon lemon juice
½ teaspoon curry powder
1 cup sharp Cheddar cheese, grated
1 cup soft bread crumbs
2 tablespoons butter
1 tablespoon olive oil

1) Place artichokes, olive oil and garlic in a 2-quart dish. Micro-cook on High power 8-10 minutes. Stir two or three times to break up frozen artichokes.
2) Drain juices and arrange artichokes in a 3-quart casserole dish.
3) Combine soup, milk, mayonnaise, lemon juice and curry powder in a 1-quart container. Mix well.

Continued on next page

4) Spread the diced chicken over the artichokes. Pour the soup mixture over all. Sprinkle on cheese.
5) Place butter in a small glass container and melt on High power 20-30 seconds.
6) Mix bread crumbs with butter. Spread over top of artichoke dish. Micro-cook on High power 8-10 minutes.

My cooking time _____

Zesty Chicken Casserole

Serves 4–6

Chicken mix

2	cups cooked chicken, cut into bite-size pieces	2	tomatoes, sliced
1	6 oz. pkg. Fritos chips	1	cup Cheddar cheese, shredded

1) In a 10″ baking dish, layer in sequence, half the chips, half the chicken and one sliced tomato.
2) Make a second layer using the same sequence of ingredients.

Sauce

1	10¾ oz. can cream of chicken soup	1	cup Cheddar cheese, shredded
½	cup water	2	teaspoons chopped chilies
1	teaspoon instant onion flakes		

3) Mix sauce ingredients thoroughly and pour over top layer of casserole. Cover dish with lid or plastic film.
4) Micro-cook on High power 6-7 minutes.
5) Remove cover and add cheese.
6) Micro-cook, uncovered, on 70% power 1 minute more.

My cooking time _____

Hamburger-Noodle Bake

 Serves 4

¾ lb. hamburger
¼ cup sour cream
½ cup water
2 tablespoons onion, chopped

6 cups cooked noodles
(left-overs are great)
1 10¾ oz. can mushroom
soup
salt

1) Preheat browning dish on High power 4 minutes then crumble hamburger onto dish.
2) Brown hamburger on High power 2 minutes. Stir meat and add onion.
3) Micro-cook on High power 1 minute more. Drain juice.
4) Combine noodles, sour cream, soup and water in a 1½-quart casserole dish. Mix meat in thoroughly. Salt to taste.
5) Micro-cook on High power 2-4 minutes.

Tip: Uncooked noodles may be used by adding ½ cup more water and allowing 3-4 more minutes cooking time.
If browning dish is not used, subtract the 4 minutes preheat time.

My cooking time _____

Jiffy Chicken à la King Casserole

Serves 5

2 10-12 oz. cans prepared
chicken à la king
1 8½ oz. can green peas
(drained)

Toast points or English
muffins for 5 people

1) Mix chicken à la king and peas in a 2-quart bowl. Cover with lid or plastic film.
2) Micro-cook on High power 3 minutes. Serve on toast points or English muffins.

Continued on next page

Tip: Also delicious served with precooked rice or noodles or leftover mashed potatoes. Warm in Microwave oven before serving.

My cooking time _____

Lasagna

 Serves 6–8

1 lb. ground beef	1 pkg. spaghetti sauce mix
1 15 oz. can Italian style marinara sauce	8 oz. lasagna noodles or wide noodles
1 8 oz. can tomato sauce	1 8 oz. pkg. thin-sliced Mozzarella cheese
1 can water (tomato sauce can)	½ cup Parmesan cheese, grated
1 cup Ricotta cheese	

1) Preheat browning dish on High power 4 minutes.
2) Crumble meat onto browning dish. Brown meat on High power. Micro-cook until meat is brown. Stir often.
3) In a large mixing bowl, combine marinara sauce, tomato sauce, water and spaghetti sauce. Add browned meat. Stir and then cover with paper towel.
4) Micro-cook on High power 10 minutes. Stir twice.
5) *While meat and sauces are cooking, cook noodles on conventional cooktop in boiling salted water until tender.* Drain and rinse in cold water.
6) Place half the noodles in 11½″ × 7½″ baking dish. Cover with half the meat sauce. Add half the ricotta, then half the mozzarella. Repeat the layers, ending with the sauce. Top with parmesan cheese.
7) Micro-cook on High power 7 minutes. Rotate dish after 3½ minutes.
8) Allow to after-cook 10 minutes.

Tip: Can be made ahead of time, covered and refrigerated. Reheat on High power 5-6 minutes.

My cooking time _____

Squash 'N Hamburger Medley   Serves 4

2 Acorn or Summer squash
   (total about 2½ lbs.)
1 lb. lean ground meat
¼ cup finely chopped onions
1 teaspoon seasoning salt
1 teaspoon Worcestershire
   sauce

½ teaspoon garlic salt or 1
   small, crushed garlic clove
4 ½ inch cubes of Cheddar or
   Monterey Jack cheese
   catsup
   salt and pepper to taste

1) Rinse squash and pierce with long-tined fork two or three times.
2) Place squash on microwave roasting rack and micro-cook on
    High power 10-12 minutes. Rotate once.
3) While squash are micro-cooking, *lightly brown ground meat in
    a skillet on cooktop. Add onion, Worcestershire sauce and sea-
    sonings. Saute 2-3 minutes more. Set aside. Don't over-cook.*
4) When squash is cooked, slice each in half, scoop out seeds and
    fill with ground meat (about ¼ cup in each squash). Place a
    cheese cube in each center, pushing it into ground meat. Add
    another ¼ cup ground meat over each squash half. Garnish
    with a ribbon of catsup.
5) Micro-cook squash on High power 4-6 minutes.
6) Tent with aluminum foil and allow to after-cook 10 minutes.

My cooking time _____

Stuffed Green Peppers   Serves 6

Meat mixture

1 lb. ground beef
½ pkg. Lipton onion soup (dry)
1 tablespoon Worcestershire
   sauce

6 pcs. bacon, cooked and
   crumbled (micro-cook on
   High power 5-6 minutes)
   dash of garlic salt
   salt and pepper

Continued on next page   69

1) Mix all ingredients in a medium-size bowl. Salt and pepper to taste. Set aside.

Sauce

2	tablespoons bacon fat (saved from cooked bacon)	1	16 oz. can tomatoes and juice
3	tablespoons flour	½	teaspoon crushed oregano
2	tablespoons brown sugar	1	8 oz. can tomato sauce

2) Combine sauce ingredients, in sequence, into a 4-cup glass container.

Peppers

6   medium green peppers, cut off tops and scoop out centers with spoon or knife

3) Place peppers in 7½" × 11½" dish or 10" casserole dish with lid.
4) Spoon meat mixture into peppers. Pour half of sauce over stuffed peppers. Cover with lid or plastic film.
5) Micro-cook on High power 8 minutes.
6) Pour on remaining sauce. Micro-cook on High power 8-10 minutes more until peppers are soft.
7) Allow to after-cook 10-15 minutes.

Tip: For softer texture of green peppers, pre-cook them in a covered dish with 2 tablespoons water on High power 3-5 minutes.

My cooking time _____

Clam Casserole

⏱ Serves 4–6

1	9 oz. can minced clams, including juice	8	large mushrooms, sliced thin
1	10½ oz. can mushroom soup	1	medium onion, chopped
		¼	teaspoon tabasco sauce

1 cup sour cream or lowfat yogurt	¼ teaspoon curry powder
¼ cup white wine	½ cup grated Cheddar cheese
2 tablespoons butter	1 10 oz. pkg. noodles
	salt to taste

1) Saute onions and mushrooms in butter on High power 2-4 minutes. Stir two to three times.
2) *Bring salted water to boil on conventional cooktop in a 3-quart sauce pan. Cook noodles until soft.*
3) Mix all ingredients except noodles and cheese in a medium mixing bowl.
4) In a 2-quart glass baking dish, spread half the noodles and cover with half the soup mixture. Layer on the remaining noodles and cover with the remaining soup mixture.
5) Micro-cook on High power 5-7 minutes.
6) Place cheese on top and micro-cook on 70% power 30-60 seconds until cheese is almost melted.
7) Cover with plastic film and allow to after-cook 5 minutes.

My cooking time _____

Patti's Red Snapper Special    Serves 6–8

1 large onion, chopped	1 2 oz. jar sliced pimientos
1 large green pepper, chopped	¼ cup tomato sauce
1 tablespoon butter	2 lbs. red snapper fillets
1 tablespoon olive oil	½ cup white wine
2 cups uncooked long-grained rice	1 tablespoon lemon juice
4 cups chicken broth (3 10½ oz. cans)	1 cup sour cream or lowfat plain yogurt
⅛ teaspoon saffron	cayenne pepper
1 teaspoon salt	parsley

1) In a 3 quart container, with lid, saute onions and green pepper in butter and olive oil. Use High power 2-3 minutes or until butter is soft.

Continued on next page

2) Add rice to onions and green peppers, stir and micro-cook on High power 2 minutes more. Set container aside.
3) In a 4-cup measure place chicken broth and saffron. Heat on High power 3-4 minutes until broth is hot.
4) Stir broth into rice mixture. Add salt, pimientos and tomato sauce and stir. Cover container and micro-cook on 50% power 20-25 minutes. Stir once. Allow to after-cook while fish is poaching.
5) Place fish in a 2-quart baking dish (7½" × 11½"). Fold each fillet in half, placing fold to outside of dish.
6) Pour wine and lemon juice evenly over fish. Cover fish with wax paper or plastic film and micro-cook on High power 5-7 minutes until fish flakes easily with a fork.
7) To serve: Place rice on a large platter. Layer fish evenly over rice. Spoon sour cream or yogurt evenly down center of fish. Sprinkle with cayenne pepper. Tent with plastic film and heat on 70% power 2-3 minutes. Garnish with parsley.

Tip: Sole and halibut are also good with this recipe.

My cooking time _____

Salmon Quiche

Serves 6–8

1 pre-baked 10″ pie crust (See ALL PURPOSE PIE CRUST recipe)

1 cup Cheddar cheese, shredded	1 10½ oz. can cream of mushroom soup, undiluted
1 1 lb. can salmon, drained	¾ cup lowfat, plain yogurt
1 tablespoon flour	1 teaspoon dill weed
2 tablespoons butter or margarine	⅛ teaspoon pepper
6 green onions, chopped, tops included	2 eggs, slightly beaten

1) Sprinkle half of cheese into pastry shell.
2) Remove bone and skin from salmon. Break salmon into chunks. Mix lightly with flour and put in pastry shell.

3) Place butter in a 1-quart measure and melt on High power 20-30 seconds.
4) Add onions to butter and micro-cook on High power 1-2 minutes until onions are soft.
5) Add soup, dill and pepper and micro-cook on High power 3-4 minutes until liquid boils. Stir in egg yolks and micro-cook on High power 1 minute more.
6) Mix in yogurt and pour over salmon. Sprinkle remaining cheese on top. Micro-cook on 70% power 10-12 minutes. Rotate dish twice. Quiche should be almost set at end of micro-cooking time.
7) Allow to after-cook 10 minutes.

My cooking time _____

Crustless Quiche Lorraine Serves 6

1	cup (4 oz.) shredded Swiss cheese	⅛	teaspoon cayenne pepper
¼	cup minced onions	10	pcs. crisp bacon, crumbled (micro-cook 5 pcs. at a time on a paper plate between double paper towels on High power 4-4½ minutes)
4	eggs		
1	13 oz. can evaporated milk		
¾	teaspoon salt		
¼	teaspoon sugar		

1) Sprinkle bacon, cheese and onion in a 9" glass pie plate.
2) Beat remaining ingredients until well blended. Pour over bacon mixture.
3) Micro-cook on 50% power 12-15 minutes. Turn dish one fourth turn every 3 minutes.
4) Allow to after-cook 10 minutes before slicing.

My cooking time _____

Baked Beans Au Chocolat

Serves 6–8

2	cups white beans (1 lb.)	¼	cup dark brown sugar
6	cups water	2	tablespoons molasses
½	lb. bacon	½	teaspoon dry mustard
¾	cup onion, chopped	¼	teaspoon pepper
1	cup barbecue sauce	⅛	teaspoon ground cloves
¼	cup instant cocoa		

1) *Place water and beans in a 3-quart container and boil for 5 minutes on conventional cooktop.* Remove from cooktop and let set one hour.
2) Cut bacon into one-inch pieces. Place bacon and onions in 2½ quart casserole with lid. Saute on High power 4-5 minutes. Stir two or three times. When ready, bacon will be limp and onions slightly soft.
3) Mix in remaining ingredients (except beans), blending well.
4) Drain beans, reserving 3 cups of bean liquid.
5) Mix beans and reserved liquid with other ingredients in the 2½ quart casserole. Micro-cook on 50% power 90 minutes, covered. Stir 3 or 4 times.
6) Allow to after-cook 10-15 minutes.

My cooking time _____

Ted's Beans

Serves 6

1½	lb. ham hock or ham scraps or ½ lb. bacon or 3 smoked Italian sausages	6	cups water
		2	chicken boullion cubes
2	cups white beans		tabasco sauce

1) *Place beans and water in 3-quart dish. Boil on conventional cooktop for 5 minutes.*
2) Remove from cooktop and let stand 1 hour.

3) Add meat, boullion cubes and 3 drops tabasco sauce.
4) Micro-cook on 50% power 80-90 minutes. Stir 3 to 4 times.
5) Allow to after-cook 10 minutes.

My cooking time _____

The Casserole

Serves 6–8

1 pkg. frozen lima beans	2 tablespoons flour
1 pkg. frozen French style green beans	1 teaspoon salt
	1 teaspoon onion flakes
1 4 oz. can mushrooms, drained	¾ teaspoon prepared mustard
¼ cup slivered almonds, toasted	2 pcs. bacon, cooked, crumbled
2 tablespoons butter	¼ cup sharp Cheddar cheese, grated

1) Pierce pouch or box of lima beans and green beans twice. Micro-cook on High power 6 minutes for lima beans and 7-8 minutes for green beans. Shake pouches well and set aside.
2) Melt butter in 4-cup measure on High power 20-30 seconds.
3) Stir flour into butter until it becomes a smooth paste. Add milk slowly, stirring well. Micro-cook on High power 3-4 minutes until thick.
4) Add salt, onion flakes and mustard. Stir until well blended. Set aside.
5) Mix vegetables, mushrooms and nuts in a 6" × 10" casserole. Spread evenly in dish. Pour sauce over vegetables evenly. Sprinkle bacon and cheese over all.
6) Micro-cook on 70% power 4-6 minutes.
7) Cover with plastic film and allow to after-cook 5-10 minutes.

My cooking time _____

Artichokes

🕑 Serves 4

4	medium artichokes, washed	garlic powder
	cooking oil	seasonings of your choice

1) Snip off leaves of artichokes and trim bottoms so that they sit flat. Rub with lemon juice.
2) Place artichokes in a 2-quart dish with lid. Sprinkle on a little oil and your seasonings.
3) Micro-cook on High power 6 minutes. Rotate dish, then micro-cook on High power 5-7 minutes more.
4) Serve with your favorite sauce, mayonnaise or lemon butter.

My cooking time _____

Asparagus

🕑 Serves 2–4

1 lb. bunch of asparagus, remove lower stems
2 tablespoons water

76

1) Lay asparagus spears in a shallow container and add water. Cover with lid or plastic wrap.
2) Micro-cook on High power 3½ minutes. Stir spears.
3) Micro-cook on High power 3½-4 minutes more.

My cooking time _____

Chuck Wagon Beans

 Serves 6

2	1-lb. cans of pork and beans (4 cups)	¼ cup barbecue sauce
¼	cup brown sugar	1 small can crushed pineapple with juice

1) Mix all ingredients in a 2-quart microwave useable bean pot with lid.
2) Micro-cook on 30% power 40 minutes. Keep covered until served.

My cooking time _____

Broccoli

 Serves 4

1 (1 lb.) bunch broccoli, rinsed and cut into bite-size pieces (cut stem into pieces also)
2 tablespoons water

Place broccoli in 1-quart container with lid. Add water and micro-cook on High power 3½ minutes. Stir and micro-cook on High power 3½-4 minutes more.

My cooking time _____

Broccoli Ring

 Serves 6–8

2	10 oz. pkgs. frozen, chopped broccoli	4	eggs, well beaten
1	cup Cheddar cheese, grated	½	cup almonds, slivered
1	small onion, chopped fine	¼	lb. fresh mushrooms, sliced
1	clove garlic, crushed	¼	cup Bisquick
2	tablespoons butter	1	teaspoon salt
			dash of pepper

1) Puncture broccoli boxes with fork tines. Place boxes in micro-wave oven and partially micro-cook on High power 4-6 minutes. Drain well in a colander.
2) Place butter in 1-quart container and melt on High power 20-30 seconds. Saute onion, garlic, and mushrooms in butter on High power 3 minutes. Stir once.
3) Combine broccoli, cheese, almonds, Bisquick and seasonings into onion-mushroom mixture. Stir in eggs. Blend well.
4) Grease well a 2-quart ring mold. Pour broccoli mixture into mold. Micro-cook on 70% power 10-12 minutes until mixture appears set and pulls away from side of mold.
5) Allow to after-cook 5 minutes. Unmold onto platter.

My cooking time _____

Cabbage

Serves 3–4

1	head cabbage, red or white, rinsed and cut into wedges	2	tablespoons water
			butter and salt

1) Place cabbage in 1-quart container. Add water, cover, and micro-cook on High power 3½ minutes. Stir and micro-cook on High power 3½-4½ minutes more.
2) Butter and salt to taste.

Tip: When cutting cabbage wedges, leave a portion of the heart on each wedge. You will be able to serve it more easily and it will look more appealing as the leaves will stay together.

My cooking time _____

Party Cauliflower

⏱ Serves 4–6

1 medium head cauliflower
3 slices American cheese

1) Rinse cauliflower well and place in a container that has a lid. Add 2 tablespoons water. Cover.
2) Micro-cook on High power 4 minutes. Rotate cauliflower and micro-cook on High power 3½ minutes more.
3) Place cheese slices over cauliflower and micro-cook on 70% power 30-45 seconds to melt cheese.

My cooking time _____

Carrots and Currants

⏱ Serves 4–6

5 medium carrots, peeled and cut into ½ inch pieces	**2 tablespoons dry vermouth**
	2 tablespoons brown sugar
¼ cup currants	**2 tablespoons butter**

Place carrots in a 1-quart container with lid. Add currants, vermouth, brown sugar and butter. Micro-cook on High power 4½ minutes. Stir and micro-cook on High power 4-5½ minutes more.

My cooking time _____

Orange-Ginger Glazed Carrots

⏱ Serves 4–6

Carrots

3½ cups carrots (1½ lbs.) cut into diagonal pieces ½ inch long	**1 tablespoon butter**
	2 tablespoons brown sugar

Continued on next page

1) Place carrots in a 1½-quart container. Top with butter and brown sugar. Cover with lid or plastic film.
2) Micro-cook on High power 5 minutes. Stir and micro-cook on High power 3 minutes more.

Glaze

½ **cup orange juice**
¼ **teaspoon salt**
1½ **tablespoon cornstarch**

¼ **teaspoon ground ginger**
dash of nutmeg

3) Mix orange juice and cornstarch in a 2-cup glass measure. Add remaining ingredients. Micro-cook on High power 1½-2 minutes. Stir twice.
4) Pour over carrots.

My cooking time _____

Celery Root

CELERIAC

Serves 4–5

1 **medium celery root**
2 **tablespoons margarine**

4 **tablespoons fruit juice**

1) Peel celery root and cut into pieces the size of French fried potatoes.
2) Place all ingredients in a 1-quart container with lid. Micro-cook on High power 4 minutes. Stir and micro-cook on High power 3 minutes more until fork tender.

My cooking time _____

Corn-On-The-Cob

Serves 1 person per cob

As many corn cobs as desired

1) Check corn for bad spots. Cut off tip. It is better to leave husk on, but if husk is removed, wrap corn loosely in plastic film.

2) Micro-cook on High power 2½-3½ minutes per cob or 6-7 minutes per pound. Rotate cobs after first 4 minutes.
3) Serve with butter. (Corn stays hotter longer than most vegetables.)

Tip: When the husk is left on, the silk can be removed easily after cooking.

My cooking time _____

Concombres Cuits
CUCUMBER

⏱ Serves 6–8

4-5	**fresh, firm cucumbers**	**1**	**tablespoon parsley, chopped**
1	**tablespoon butter**		**(optional)**

1) Peel cucumbers and slice into quarters. Scoop out seeds. Cut into 3-inch pieces.
2) Place butter and cucumbers in a covered glass dish and micro-cook on High power 5-6 minutes.
3) Sprinkle with parsley before serving.

My cooking time _____

Gado-Gado
STEAMED VEGETABLES WITH PEANUT SAUCE

⏱ Serves 4

Vegetables

4	**leaves of cabbage**	**8**	**fresh asparagus or 8 fresh**
8	**large spinach leaves,**		**green beans, snapped**
	deveined (take center stem	**8-12**	**tablespoons bean sprouts**
	out)	**1**	**egg, hard boiled**

1) Spread the cabbage leaves on a plate. On each leaf place 2 spinach leaves, 2 asparagus and 2-3 tablespoons of bean sprouts. Cover with plastic film.

Continued on next page 81

2) Micro-cook on High power 4-5 minutes. Garnish with sliced egg.

Peanut Sauce

1	clove garlic, crushed	2	tablespoons soy sauce
1	small onion, chopped	1	tablespoon lemon juice
1	red chili pepper	5	oz. peanut butter
⅛	teaspoon ground cumin	½	teaspoon sugar
½	teaspoon ground ginger	¾	cup canned coconut milk
1	tablespoon peanut oil		

3) In a 1-quart container, saute chili pepper, cumin and ginger in the peanut oil on High power 45 seconds.
4) Add remaining ingredients and micro-cook on High power 30-60 seconds more. Serve in a sauce boat.

My cooking time _____

Green Beans Special

Serves 6

2	17 oz. cans green beans, drained	½	cup milk
1	10½ oz. can cream of mushroom soup	1	3 oz. can French fried dry onions

1) Mix all ingredients well in a 1½ quart casserole.
2) Cover with paper towel and micro-cook on High power 4-6 minutes.

My cooking time _____

Green Beans with Toasted Almonds

Serves 2–4

½ cup blanched almonds
1 10 oz. can French style green beans

1) Place almonds in shallow container. Micro-cook on High power 4-5 minutes until toasted.
2) Mix in beans and cover. Micro-cook on High power 3-4 minutes more.

My cooking time _____

Mushrooms

Serves 4–5

½ lb. mushrooms, rinsed and patted dry
2 tablespoons butter

2-3 tablespoons chopped onions
salt and pepper

1) Cut mushroom stems into 3 to 4 pieces.
2) Place butter in 1-quart container and melt on High power 20-30 seconds.
3) Add mushroom caps and cut stems. Cover container with lid or plastic film. Micro-cook on High power 2 minutes.
4) Stir in onions. Micro-cook on High power 4-6 minutes. Salt and pepper to taste.

My cooking time _____

Onions

🕐 Serves 2–4

1-2 onions, peeled and cut into ¼″ thick slices
1 tablespoon butter

1) Place butter and onions in a 1-quart container. Cover with plastic film or lid.
2) Micro-cook on High power: 1 medium onion 3½-4 minutes; 2 medium onions 4½-5 minutes, or to doneness desired.

Tip: These are especially delicious with hamburgers or meat loaf. Red onions make a very eye-appealing dish.

My cooking time _____

Best *En Concert* White Onions 🕐🕐 Serves 6–8

2 lbs. small, white boiling onions or 2 pkgs. frozen onions
⅓ cup butter

¼ teaspoon white pepper
2 teaspoons fresh parsle‡, chopped

1) Place onions and 3 tablespoons water in a 2-quart dish with lid. Micro-cook on High power 3-4 minutes. Allow to aftercook 5 minutes. Peel while warm.
2) Cut a small round hole in the base of each onion. Place onions in 9″ × 13″ glass baking dish. Dot with butter, sprinkle with pepper and cover with plastic film. Micro-cook on High power 5-7 minutes until fork tender. Stir twice.
3) Uncover onions. *Place dish in conventional oven preheated to 350°F for 10 minutes until onions are slightly brown.* Garnish with parsley and serve.

Tip: Can be cooked early and reheated on High power 4-5 minutes, stirring twice while reheating.

My cooking time _____

En Concert Oven-Braised Parsnips with Brussels Sprouts

Serves 6–8

4	large parsnips, peeled and quartered	¼	teaspoon white pepper
¼	cup brown sugar	⅛	teaspoon salt
3	tablespoons butter	1½	lbs. Brussels sprouts (about 4 cups) trimmed and rinsed
4	tablespoons water		

1) Place parsnips in 2-quart dish with lid. Micro-cook on High power 8-10 minutes until fork tender.
2) Arrange parsnips in 7½″ × 11½″ dish. Sprinkle with brown sugar, salt and pepper and dot with butter.
3) *Bake, uncovered, in a pre-heated conventional oven at 350°F 15-20 minutes until sugar is melted and parsnips are glazed.*
4) While parsnips are cooking, place Brussels sprouts and water in a covered 10″ glass baking dish. Micro-cook on High power 7-9 minutes. Stir twice.
5) Arrange parsnips and Brussels sprouts on a platter and serve hot.

Tip: Both vegetables may be cooked early and reheated. If this is done, reheat them separately. Both on High power—3-4 minutes for parsnips—2-3 minutes for Brussels sprouts.

My cooking time _____

Parslied Potatoes

Serves 4–6

3	medium baking potatoes, peeled, rinsed and sliced evenly or,	1	tablespoon chopped chives
		2	tablespoons chopped parsley
5	small new red potatoes, scrubbed, rinsed and sliced evenly	2	tablespoons butter

Continued on next page 85

1) Place potatoes in 2-quart container with lid.
2) Micro-cook on High power 8-9 minutes until fork tender. Shake dish after first 3 minutes.
3) Add remaining ingredients and micro-cook on High power 45-60 seconds more.
4) Shake dish well and allow to after-cook 3-5 minutes.

Tip: Delicious with ham, lamb or pork roast.

My cooking time _____

Scalloped Potatoes

 Serves 4–6

5   medium potatoes, sliced evenly, about ⅛-inch thick
3½ tablespoons flour
1   teaspoon salt
2   tablespoons butter

1¼ cup scalded milk (scald in 2-cup measure on High power 75-90 seconds)
paprika

1) Place half the potatoes in a 2-quart container with lid.
2) Mix flour and salt and sprinkle half over potatoes.
3) Place remaining potatoes in dish and sprinkle remaining flour and salt mixture over them.
4) Pour scalded milk over all. Sprinkle with paprika and dot with butter.
5) Cover with lid or plastic film and micro-cook on High power 12-14 minutes until potatoes are tender. Rotate dish after 6 minutes.
6) Allow to after-cook 15-20 minutes.

My cooking time _____

Zippy Hash Browns

Serves 4

3   large potatoes
2   tablespoons chopped onions

butter, margarine or bacon grease
salt and pepper

1) Micro-cook potatoes on High power 11-13 minutes. Allow to after-cook 5 minutes. Peel and dice.
2) *Preheat skillet on conventional cooktop.*
3) *Place small amount of butter in skillet. Add onions. Salt and pepper to taste.*
4) *Add potatoes and allow them to brown while remainder of meal is prepared.*

Tip: Cook potatoes the night before. Pop them into microwave oven on your way to bed. They will be ready and waiting in the morning.

My cooking time _____

Sugar 'N Spice Yams

 Serves 4

1 **lb. yams (3 medium size)**	1 **tablespoon instant cocoa**
2 **tablespoons butter**	2 **tablespoons Grand Marnier**
½ **teaspoon salt**	**or brandy**
½ **cup dark corn syrup**	¼ **cup pecan halves**
½ **teaspoon pumpkin spice**	

1) Place butter in 10″ glass baking dish. Melt on High power 20-30 seconds.
2) Peel yams and cut into slices ½ inch thick.
3) Place yam slices in melted butter, and coat all sides. Cover dish and micro-cook on High power 3 minutes.
4) In a small glass measure blend syrup, pumpkin spice, cocoa and Grand Marnier and pour over yams. Sprinkle with pecans.
5) Cover and micro-cook on High power 4-6 minutes until fork tender.
6) Allow to after-cook 5 minutes.

My cooking time _____

Sweet Potato Soufflé

3 eggs, separated
1 cup milk
1 teaspoon salt
2 tablespoons butter
3-4 tablespoons water

3 lbs. sweet potatoes, cut into
1-inch pieces
1 10 oz. pkg. frozen peas
walnut halves
brown sugar

1) Butter a 12-cup bundt cake dish or a ring mold generously. Arrange walnut halves around bottom of dish and sprinkle with brown sugar. Set dish aside.
2) Place potatoes in a 3-quart container, add water and micro-cook on High power 16 minutes. Stir every 5 minutes.
3) Allow potatoes to after-cook 5-10 minutes then mash well.
4) While potatoes are cooking and after-cooking, beat egg whites until stiff and melt butter on High power 20-30 seconds in a small container.
5) After potatoes have after-cooked, add butter, milk, salt and egg yolks. Blend well. Fold in egg whites.
6) Gently place mixture in mold, piling it evenly. Micro-cook on High power 10-12 minutes. Rotate mold every 3 minutes Micro-cook until a toothpick comes out clean.
7) Allow soufflé to after-cook 5-10 minutes then unmold onto a platter.
8) While soufflé is after-cooking, puncture the package of peas with fork. Place package in microwave oven and micro-cook on High power 5 minutes. Pour peas into center of soufflé and dot with butter.

Tip: A soufflé reheats beautifully if kept well-covered and refrigerated. Reheat on High power 3-5 minutes.

My cooking time _____

Spinach

 Serves 2 people per bunch

Number of bunches of spinach desired
butter and lemon juice

1) Clean and rinse leaves, allowing water droplets to remain. Break leaves into small pieces and place in a 1-quart container with lid.
2) Micro-cook on High power: 1 bunch 1½-2 minutes; 2 bunches 2-3½ minutes. Stir after 1-2 minutes.
3) Season with butter and lemon juice.

My cooking time _____

Squash, Acorn

 Serves 2 people per medium squash

1   medium squash   **brown sugar**
    butter

1) Wash squash. Puncture skin with fork tines. Place squash in microwave oven. No container is needed.
2) Micro-cook on High power 4 minutes.
3) Cut squash in half and remove seeds. Micro-cook on High power 3½-4½ minutes more. Add butter and brown sugar during last few seconds of cooking.

Tip: When cooking squash without a container, place a glass with ½ to ¾ inch of water in corner of microwave oven to add a little moisture.

My cooking time _____

Squash, Banana

⏱ Serves 2–3

½ of a 1 lb. banana squash
1 teaspoon butter

salt and pepper

1) Wash squash and remove seeds.
2) Place in a covered container or cover squash with plastic film.
3) Micro-cook on High power 7½-8½ minutes. Rotate container after 4 minutes. Add salt, pepper and butter during last 45 seconds.

My cooking time _____

Tomatoes Vinaigrette

⏱ Serves 6–8

6 medium tomatoes
small jar French dressing

2 teaspoons chives, chopped
2 teaspoons parsley, chopped

1) Heat tomatoes on High power 15-20 seconds per tomato. Rub gently with hands to remove skin.
2) Slice tomatoes and place on serving dish. Sprinkle with chives and parsley then drizzle with French dressing.
3) Chill several hours before serving.

My cooking time _____

The Stuffed Tomato

⏱⏱ Serves 6

6 medium, firm tomatoes
¼ teaspoon salt
2 10 oz. pkgs. chopped frozen spinach
2 tablespoons butter
¼ teaspoon salt

⅛ teaspoon pepper
1 tablespoon fresh green onion, minced
¼ cup soft bread crumbs
¼ cup Parmesan cheese

1) Wash tomatoes and cut crosswise into halves. Scoop out centers and sprinkle inside lightly with salt. Invert halves on paper towel-lined tray to drain.
2) Puncture two holes in spinach pouch and micro-cook on High power 7-9 minutes. Allow to after-cook 5 minutes.
3) Place spinach in medium size mixing bowl and add salt, pepper, butter, onion and bread crumbs. Toss well with a fork.
4) Stuff each tomato half with filling. Sprinkle with Parmesan cheese. Place tomato halves in a dish, leaving space between each half. Cover lightly with wax paper.
5) Micro-cook on 70% power 6-8 minutes until cheese is melted and tomato can be pierced easily with a fork.
6) Allow to after-cook 5 minutes.

My cooking time _____

Zucchini

Serves 4

4 medium zucchini, cut into ½ inch pieces

Rinse and place in 1-quart container with lid. Micro-cook on High power 5½-6½ minutes. Stir after 3 minutes. Season to taste.

My cooking time _____

Zucchini Potpourri

Serves 6–8

4	small zucchini	2	tablespoons olive or Saffola
1	medium onion		oil
1	bunch spinach	⅓	cup milk
½	bell pepper	½	cup Parmesan cheese,
1	teaspoon lemon juice		grated
1	teaspoon sugar	2	cups bread cubes or crumbs,
½	teaspoon seasoning salt		dried
2	eggs, beaten	¼	cup Cheddar cheese, grated

1) Chop vegetables individually in blender or food processor.

Continued on next page 91

2) Place chopped vegetables in 2-quart mixing bowl and add lemon juice and sugar. Stir.
3) Combine in a separate dish eggs, oil, milk, Parmesan cheese and breads. Add this combination to vegetable mixture.
4) Micro-cook on High power 10-12 minutes uncovered.
5) Sprinkle with Cheddar cheese, cover. Allow to after-cook 5-10 minutes.

My cooking time _____

Meat Loaf

 Serves 4

1 lb. ground meat	½ cup bread crumbs or
½ pkg. dry onion soup mix	crumbled crackers
1 egg	1 teaspoon Worcestershire
½ teaspoon garlic salt or	sauce
powder	½ cup catsup

1) Mix all ingredients, except catsup, in 1½ quart utility dish or 4″ × 8½″ loaf dish. (Don't pack tightly and don't "mound" the meat.)
2) Make a design on top using a knife handle or wooden spoon. Pour catsup into design. Cover meat with paper towel.
3) Micro-cook on High power 11-12 minutes. Rotate dish after 6 minutes.

My cooking time _____

Saucy Patties

 Serves 4–6

1 lb. lean ground meat	3 green onions, diced
½ cup bread crumbs	2 carrots, diced
2 tablespoons milk	1 10¾ oz. can cream of
3 ribs celery, diced	chicken soup

Continued on next page   93

1) Mix ground meat, bread crumbs and milk and form into patties.
2) Preheat browning dish on High power 4 minutes. Place patties on dish and brown on High power 1 minute. Turn patties over and brown on High power 3 minutes more.
3) Spoon diced vegetables over patties, then spoon soup over all. Cover with lid or plastic film.
4) Micro-cook on High power 10 minutes. Rotate dish twice.

Tip: The vegetables in this dish may be varied to your taste.

My cooking time _____

Pot Roast 'N Vegetables

Serves 4–6

Roast

2	cups favorite marinade	1	medium onion, sliced thick
1	4 lb. chuck roast	3	potatoes, peeled and sliced
1	pkg. Lipton's onion soup	2	ribs celery, chopped
3	medium carrots, sliced in ½ inch pieces		

1) Marinate roast 1 hour in marinade.
2) Place roast, onion soup, carrots and 1 cup marinade in 3-quart dish with lid. Micro-cook on High power 8 minutes.
3) Micro-cook on 50% power 40 minutes. After 25 minutes, rotate roast and add remaining vegetables. Cook until vegetables become fork tender. When nearing completion, test vegetables every 60 seconds.
4) Remove from microwave oven and place meat and vegetables on another dish while preparing gravy.

Gravy

	roast juices	¼	cup cold water
3	tablespoons cornstarch		

5) Add cornstarch and water to roast juices.
6) Micro-cook on High power, stirring every 45 seconds, until gravy consistency is as desired.
7) Place meat and vegetables back into cooking dish and spoon gravy over meat to create a glaze.
8) Serve immediately or refrigerate until serving time. Reheat on High power 3-5 minutes in covered dish.

My cooking time _____

Delicious Flank Steak  Serves 4–6

¼	cup butter or margarine	½	teaspoon oregano
¼	cup sesame seeds	1	teaspoon Worcestershire
½	cup chopped celery		sauce
3	tablespoons chopped onions	2	flank steaks, 1-1½ lbs. each
3	slices bread, cubed	1	cup water
1	teaspoon salt	1	cube beef bouillon

1) Combine butter, sesame seeds, celery and onions in medium-size mixing bowl. Micro-cook on High power 1 minute or until butter melts.
2) Add bread, salt, oregano and Worcestershire sauce, mixing well.
3) Score both sides of each steak, diagonally, about 1 inch apart.
4) Place half of stuffing down center of each steak, lengthwise. Roll and tie each steak with string.
5) Place both steaks, seam side down, in 7½" × 11½" baking dish. Fill dish with water and add bouillon cube. Cover dish with wax paper or heavy plastic film.
6) Micro-cook on 50% power 40-45 minutes. Turn steaks over halfway through cooking time.
7) Allow to after-cook 10 minutes.

My cooking time _____

Parmesan-Crusted Round Steak ⏲⏲ Serves 6–8

Round Steak

1	2 lb. round steak about ¾" thick (size to fit browning dish)	1	teaspoon instant coffee
½	tablespoon salad oil	1	tablespoon dry, minced onion
1	tablespoon flour	2	tablespoons red wine
			paprika, salt, pepper, Accent

1) Preheat browning dish on High power 5 minutes. Add salad oil.
2) Mix flour, coffee and paprika in small container and rub into both sides of meat.
3) Place meat in browning dish and micro-cook on High power 3 minutes. Turn meat over, cover with lid and micro-cook on High power 2 minutes more.
4) Add seasonings, onion and wine. (If meat is making too much juice, omit the wine.) Micro-cook on 70% power 10-12 minutes more until fork tender.

Parmesan Mixture

2   tablespoons mayonnaise
½ cup Parmesan cheese, grated

5) Stir cheese into mayonnaise until mixture becomes very thick. (It takes about ½ cup of cheese.)
6) *Preheat conventional broiler. When meat is tender, place it on oven-proof platter. Spread Parmesan mixture over meat. Broil until cheese becomes puffed and bubbles.*

My cooking time _____

Fabulous Stew

😊😊😊 Serves 4–6

2½ lb. stew meat cut into 1½-inch pieces	¼ teaspoon oregano
1 pkg. dry onion soup	¼ teaspoon caraway seeds
1 teaspoon brown sugar	1 12 oz. can "flat" beer
2 teaspoons vinegar	1½ tablespoons prepared mustard
1 bay leaf, crumbled	1 slice crusty French bread

1) Place meat in a 3-quart casserole dish. Add onion soup and cover with lid.
2) Micro-cook on High power 8 minutes. Stir and micro-cook on 50% power 16 minutes more.
3) Add remaining dry ingredients, mixing well, then add beer. Beer should just cover the meat.
4) Spread mustard on both sides French bread. Cut bread in half and place on meat mixture, pressing bread lightly into liquid.
5) Replace lid and micro-cook on 50% power 45-60 minutes. Mash bread into stew. When done, meat should be fork tender.

Tip: For beer to become "flat," let an open can stand for an hour or more. Another method is to pour beer into a container and beat with a fork until no more bubbles appear.

My cooking time _____

Veal Paprika

😊 Serves 5

1 lb. veal steak, cut into 2-inch pieces	1 10¾ oz. can mushroom soup
¼ cup seasoned flour	½ soup can of white wine
1 tablespoon oil	1 tablespoon paprika

1) Coat veal with seasoned flour. (Paprika, garlic salt, pepper and seasoning salt.)
2) Preheat browning dish on High power 4½ minutes.

Continued on next page 97

3) Place oil and meat on browning dish. Micro-cook on High power 6 minutes. Stir every 2 minutes.
4) Add soup, wine and paprika. Stir well.
5) Micro-cook on 70% power 4-5 minutes more. Stir every 2½ minutes.
6) Serve over cooked noodles.

My cooking time _____

Cranberry-Glazed Ham

Serves 10-12

    1   **4-5 lb. precooked ham**
    1   **8 oz. can jellied cranberries**

1) Place ham in flat dish on microwave roasting rack. Micro-cook on 70% power 12 minutes.
2) Turn ham over and spread cranberry jelly over top and sides. Micro-cook on 70% power 10-12 minutes more.
3) Allow to after-cook 10-15 minutes covered before carving.

My cooking time _____

Baked Ginger Pork Chops

Serves 4-5

5	**shoulder pork chops**	**¼**	**teaspoon cinnamon**
2	**teaspoons Accent**	**⅛**	**teaspoon pepper**
¼	**teaspoon orange peel**	**¼**	**teaspoon allspice**
½	**teaspoon fresh-grated ginger root**	**1**	**cup chicken broth**
			dash of onion powder
¼	**teaspoon thyme .**		

1) *Brown pork chops in skillet on conventional cooktop. Place them in a 7½" × 11½" dish.*

2) Mix remaining ingredients. Pour over pork chops.
3) Micro-cook on 70% power 8-10 minutes until pork chops are fork tender and juice runs clear when chops are pierced.

My cooking time _____

Hawaiian Ribs

 Serves 4-6

Ribs

4 lbs. country style spareribs	¼ teaspoon pepper
¼ cup flour	¼ teaspoon seasoning salt
½ teaspoon paprika	

1) Cut ribs into serving size pieces. Pat with paper towel.
2) Mix all ingredients except ribs in paper bag. Shake 2 ribs at a time in flour mixture. Set ribs aside.

Sauce

1 can crushed pineapple (6 oz.)	1 tablespoon brown sugar
¼ cup apricot jam	1 tablespoon lemon juice
3 tablespoon teriyaki sauce	1 tablespoon sherry wine
1 teaspoon Worcestershire sauce	½ teaspoon powdered ginger
	½ teaspoon onion powder
	¼ teaspoon garlic powder

3) Mix ingredients together in a 1-quart container to form sauce.
4) Place floured ribs in shallow baking dish. Spoon ⅓ cup of sauce over ribs.
5) Micro-cook on 70% power 20 minutes. Turn ribs once.
6) Drain and discard liquid.
7) Pour remaining sauce over ribs and micro-cook on 70% power 10-14 minutes more until ribs are tender and brown. Turn ribs and baste twice.
8) Allow ribs to after-cook 10-15 minutes.

My cooking time _____

Saucy Spareribs

3½ lbs. country-style spareribs (cut by butcher for ease of serving)	1 8¼ oz. can crushed pineapple
	½ cup Kraft Barbecue Sauce

1) Place spareribs in covered dish and micro-cook on High power 14-16 minutes.
2) *Move spareribs to a rack in a roasting pan and broil in a conventional oven 5 to 6 inches from heat until spareribs are desired color (about 10 minutes). While ribs are broiling, baste with a mixture of the pineapple and barbecue sauce.*

My cooking time _____

Pork Loin

Serves 4-6

Sauce

½ teaspoon salt	½ cup peach chutney
½ teaspoon Accent	2 tablespoons vinegar
½ cup seedless blackberry jam	½ teaspoon ginger, ground

1) Mix ingredients together to form sauce.

Pork Loin

1 3½ lb. pork loin
½ cup walnuts, chopped

2) Place loin in 2-quart casserole dish and spread half of sauce over loin.
3) Micro-cook on 70% power 25-30 minutes. Rotate meat once.
4) Baste and pour on remaining sauce. Micro-cook on 70% power 20 minutes.
5) Add walnuts and micro-cook on 70% power 5 minutes more.
6) Let after-cook 15-20 minutes.

My cooking time _____

Pork Loin 'N Potato Bake

 Serves 6-8

3½-4 lb. pork loin, cut through
by butcher for ease of carving
2 green apples, sliced
1 10¾ oz. can sauerkraut

4 medium potatoes, peeled
and sliced lengthwise
salt and pepper

1) Place apple slice between each pork chop.
2) Place loin in 10″ casserole, fat side down. Cover with lid or plastic film.
3) Micro-cook on 70% power 24-26 minutes.
4) Drain off juices. Salt and pepper to taste. Turn loin fat side up. Add sauerkraut and potatoes.
5) Micro-cook on 70% power 21-23 minutes more, covered.

My cooking time _____

Spanish Loin of Pork

 Serves 4-6

Sauce

3 tablespoons butter
⅓ cup minced onion
1 tablespoon chili powder
dash of garlic powder
½ teaspoon salt
½ teaspoon Accent

¾ cup currants
2 8 oz. cans tomato sauce
½ cup sliced green or ripe
olives
3 tablespoons brown sugar
⅓ cup diced green pepper

1) Place butter in 1½-quart container and melt on High power 30-45 seconds. Saute onion in butter on High power 2 minutes.
2) Add remaining ingredients and micro-cook on High power 1½ minutes.
3) Refrigerate sauce until ready to serve pork loin.

Continued on next page   101

Pork Loin

1   3½ lb. pork loin, loosened from rib bone and
      cut for servings
2   cups cooked rice

4) Place meat in a 3-quart baking dish with lid. Mix one fourth of sauce with rice and stuff into loin between slices. Pour remaining sauce over meat. Cover.
5) Micro-cook on 70% power 40-45 minutes. Rotate dish twice.
6) Baste with sauce and micro-cook on High power 5 minutes more.
7) Allow to after-cook 15 minutes.

My cooking time _____

Microwave Chicken Curry   🕐🕐🕐 Serves 4–6

3   lbs. chicken parts
1   10 oz. can chicken broth
1   cup water
½   teaspoon seasoned salt
¾   cup minced fresh onion
1   clove garlic, crushed
¾   cup tart apple, grated

¼   teaspoon dry mustard
¼   teaspoon dry ginger
¼   teaspoon ground cardamom
½   teaspoon salt
¼   teaspoon pepper
1   tablespoon baking cocoa
¼   cup flour

| 4 | tablespoons butter | 1 | tablespoon lemon juice |
| 2 | teaspoons curry powder | ⅓ | cup half-and-half |

1) Place chicken parts in 9″ × 13″ glass baking dish with thickest parts of chicken to the outside edge. Micro-cook on High power 20-22 minutes. Rotate dish once.
2) Cover with wax paper and allow to after-cook 10 minutes.
3) Bone chicken parts and cut meat into bite-size pieces.
4) Place butter, onion, garlic and apple in 1-quart covered dish. Saute on High power 3-4 minutes.
5) Stir in curry, mustard, ginger, cardamom, salt, pepper, cocoa and flour. Micro-cook on 50% power 3 minutes.
6) Add lemon juice, half-and-half, chicken broth and water. Stir. Micro-cook on 70% power 6-8 minutes until sauce thickens. Stir several times while cooking.
7) Add chicken meat and stir. Micro-cook on 50% power 6-8 minutes.
8) Serve over rice, with condiments such as chutney, chopped peanuts, toasted coconut, raisins soaked in wine, diced banana, chopped cucumber and chopped green pepper.

My cooking time _____

Coconut Chicken

 Serves 3–4

| 6 | pcs. chicken (2 breasts, 2 thighs and 2 drumsticks) | ¼ | cup Coconut Snow (found in liquor section of stores) |
| ¼ | cup butter or margarine | 2 | tablespoons Trader Vic's Javanese Saté Spice |

1) Place butter in small glass dish and melt on High power 45-60 seconds.
2) Coat chicken pieces with melted butter.
3) Roll chicken in Coconut Snow then in Saté Spice.
4) Place chicken in 2-quart rectangular dish with thicker parts toward edge of dish.
5) Micro-cook on High power 24-26 minutes.
6) Allow to after-cook 10 minutes.

My cooking time _____

Drumstick Dinner

6 large chicken legs (1½ lbs.)
Shake-N-Bake Seasoning

1) Coat drumsticks with seasoning and place in a 9″ square dish or 10″ browning dish. Place thick parts of chicken toward outside edge of dish.
2) Micro-cook on High power 3½ minutes. Turn legs over and micro-cook on High power 3½-4 minutes more.
3) Allow drumsticks to after-cook 3-5 minutes.

My cooking time _____

Grenadine Chicken With Walnuts

Serves 4–6

1 cut-up fryer (3-4 lbs.)	1 lemon
¼ cup flour	¾ cup grenadine syrup
½ teaspoon pepper	2 tablespoons cornstarch
1 teaspoon each of salt and monosodium glutamate	1 cup walnuts, chopped

1) Shake chicken parts in paper bag containing mixture of flour, salt, pepper and monosodium glutamate.
2) Place chicken parts in casserole with heavier pieces to outside of dish.
3) Sprinkle chicken with juice of lemon.
4) Mix grenadine and cornstarch and pour over chicken.
5) Micro-cook on High power 18-20 minutes. Rotate dish twice.
6) Turn chicken pieces over and micro-cook on High power 5 minutes more.
7) Pour walnuts over chicken and baste chicken with walnuts and juices.

8) *Slip dish under conventional broiler for a minute or two to obtain color and bubbly effect.*
9) Allow to after-cook 10 minutes. Serve with rice.

My cooking time _____

Hong Kong Lemon Chicken ♨♨♨ Serves 4–6

3½ lbs. of chicken breasts (6-8 breasts)

Bake in batter in conventional oven at 375°F for 45-60 minutes.

Batter

½	cup flour	2	tablespoons wine vinegar
2	tablespoon sherry		

Mix ingredients using a wire whisk or fork to form a smooth batter. Pour sauce into shallow dish and dip breasts into batter. Bake. Or, dip breasts in egg batter and micro-cook on High power 20-22 minutes.

Egg Batter

2 eggs
½ cup milk

Whip eggs in shallow bowl with wire whisk or a fork until soupy. Add milk and stir to blend. Dip breasts into batter and then into cracker crumbs or dry French bread crumbs. Micro-cook.

Prepare lemon sauce while chicken is cooking

Lemon Sauce

½	medium onion, sliced thin	1½	cups chicken broth (1
2	tablespoons peanut oil		10½ oz. can)
2	tablespoons sherry	⅔	cup brown sugar
2	tablespoons soy sauce	2	tablespoons lemon juice
2	tablespoons cornstarch	2	lemons, sliced thin

Continued on next page 105

1) Heat peanut oil in High power 1-1½ minutes until hot.
2) Saute onion slices in peanut oil on High power 1 minute.
3) Stir in remaining ingredients and micro-cook on High power 2 minutes. Stir. Micro-cook on High power 3-4 minutes more until sauce is slightly thickened and glazed.
4) Pour sauce over chicken. Garnish with parsley and serve.

Tip: Chicken may be re-heated on the platter. Heat on High power 3-4 minutes.

My cooking time _____

Barbara's Potted Turkey  Serves 6–8

1 12 lb. turkey

Marinade

½ cup salad oil
½ cup bourbon
3 tablespoons soy sauce
2 teaspoons garlic powder

2 teaspoons Worcestershire sauce
dash of pepper

1) Mix marinade ingredients in a 2-cup measure.
2) Pierce turkey several times with a long-tined fork. Place turkey in large heavy plastic bag. (Sometimes two bags are better. Do not let wings poke holes in bag.)
3) Pour marinade over turkey and refrigerate overnight. Turn once. Remove from refrigerator 2 hours before cooking and allow turkey to come to room temperature.

Micro-Cooking the Turkey

4) Take turkey out of plastic bag and place on microwave roasting rack in a 2 or 3-quart rectangular dish.
5) Micro-cook on High power 7 minutes per pound. Rotate turkey every 20 minutes. (See TIP.)
6) When wing tips and lower part of drumsticks look done, shield with small pieces of foil secured in place with toothpicks.

Tip: When rotating turkey, start with breast down, then on side(s) (use a glass to prop turkey in position) then on back. Finish cooking with breast up.

My cooking time _____

Fish Charlene

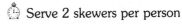 Serves 4

2	lbs. fresh cod or red snapper fillets	2	tablespoons chopped green onions (stem included)
½	cup buttermilk coarse ground pepper to taste	1	tablespoon chopped fresh parsley

1) Fold fillets in half with the fold toward the edge of the dish.
2) Pour buttermilk over fillets.
3) Sprinkle onions, pepper and parsley over fillets.
4) Cover lightly with plastic film.
5) Micro-cook on High power 5-7 minutes. When done, fish should flake easily with fork and be opaque.
6) Allow to after-cook 5 minutes.

FOR VARIATION: Substitute the following for buttermilk and seasonings: ¼ cup soy sauce, 2 tablespoons melted butter, 2 teaspoons lemon juice, 1 tablespoon chopped fresh parsley, pepper to taste.

My cooking time _____

Oysters en Brochette

Serve 2 skewers per person

1	slice very lean bacon	lemon juice
4	mushroom caps	freshly ground pepper
4	oysters, defrosted and shucked	butter

Continued on next page   107

1) Run a skewer through one end of bacon. Then, in sequence, skewer a mushroom cap, an oyster, through bacon, mushroom cap, oyster, bacon until the skewer is filled and the bacon laced through.
2) Sprinkle with lemon juice, pepper and brush with butter.
3) Arrange skewers on a round platter in wheel-spoke fashion with space between each skewer (4 to 6 skewers at a time).
4) Micro-cook on High power until bacon begins to crisp and oysters just start to curl (4-6 minutes).
5) *Remove skewers from microwave oven and place under pre-heated broiler or on barbecue to crisp (5-7 minutes).*
6) Serve with Hollandaise Sauce II recipe.

My cooking time _____

Oysters and Wild Rice

Serves 4

1½	cups oysters, defrosted and shucked (reserve liquor)	½	cup chicken broth
½	cup cooked wild rice	½	cup butter
		2	cups cracker crumbs

1) Place butter in small bowl and melt on High power 60-90 seconds. Add cracker crumbs and mix thoroughly.
2) Butter a 9″ baking dish. Arrange in the dish, in layers, half the buttered crumbs, half the rice and all the oysters. (Layer each ingredient evenly.)
3) Dot the oysters with butter and layer in remaining rice.
4) Add chicken broth to reserved oyster liquor to make 1 cup liquid. Pour this liquid over layers. Sprinkle remaining crumbs over top.
5) Cover dish with paper towel and micro-cook on High power 7-8 minutes. Rotate dish twice.
6) Remove paper towel and micro-cook on High power 2-3 minutes more.
7) Cover dish with foil and allow to after-cook 5-10 minutes. Remove foil and serve.

Tip: Oysters may be defrosted on 30% power. One pound (4 cups) of frozen, shucked oysters will defrost in 6-8 minutes. Stir once or twice while defrosting.

My cooking time _____

Scalloped Oysters

Serves 4-6

3 cups oysters, defrosted and shucked (reserve ¼ cup liquor)

2 cups cracker crumbs (46 crackers)

½ cup butter or margarine

¾ cup light cream

½ teaspoon salt

½ teaspoon Worcestershire sauce

pepper

1) Place butter in small container and melt on High power 60-90 seconds.
2) Combine cracker crumbs with butter.
3) Spread ⅓ of buttered crumbs in a round dish 9″ in diameter and 2″ deep.
4) Cover crumbs with ½ of oysters. Sprinkle with pepper. Use ⅓ of crumbs for second layer. Cover with remaining oysters.
5) Combine cream, reserved liquor, salt and Worcestershire sauce. Pour over oysters. Top with remaining crumbs.
6) Micro-cook on High power 8-10 minutes.
7) Allow to after-cook 5-10 minutes.

My cooking time _____

Joan Toole's Scampi

⏱ Serves 4–6

Prawns

2 lbs. fresh prawns, medium size
¼ cup dry sherry

Prawns can be shelled and cleaned ahead of time, wrapped in plastic and refrigerated until ready for use.

Prawn Butter

⅓ cup dry bread crumbs, small size	1½ teaspoon chives, chopped fine
½ teaspoon salt	1 teaspoon minced onions
¼ teaspoon paprika	¼ teaspoon Worcestershire sauce
2 cloves garlic, crushed	
1 teaspoon parsley, chopped fine	1 stick soft butter

Mix ingredients thoroughly, wrap in plastic. Refrigerate until solid.

1) Place cleaned prawns in 10″ dish. Add sherry. Stir.
2) Slice half of prawn butter over prawns and micro-cook on High power 4-5 minutes. Stir twice.

Tip: Freeze remaining prawn butter and use another time.

My cooking time _____

Veracruz Style Snapper

⏱ Serves 4–6

1 2½ lb. red snapper fillet	½ of 7 oz. jar stuffed green olives (cut olives in half)
1 medium onion, diced	
1 tablespoon olive oil	1 tablespoon capers
1 #2½ size can solid pack tomatoes	salt and pepper

1) Place olive oil in 1-quart container and saute onions in the oil on High power 2-3 minutes.

2) Add tomatoes, olives and capers. Salt and pepper to taste.
3) Micro-cook on High power 2 minutes.
4) Place snapper in 9″ × 13″ container. Spoon a little sauce over fish. Cover dish with plastic film. Vent a corner.
5) Micro-cook on High power 3 minutes. Pour on remaining sauce and micro-cook on High power 4-6 minutes more or until fish flakes easily with fork.
6) Allow to after-cook 5 minutes.

My cooking time _____

All Purpose Pie Crust *(9" pie)*

¾ cup shortening	1 teaspoon salt
2¼ cups flour	5 tablespoons ice water

1) Cut shortening into flour and salt mixture until mixture is fine (pea size).
2) Put ice water into small bowl and mix in ⅓ cup flour mixture, using a fork for mixing.
3) Add the flour-water mixture to remaining flour mixture and mix thoroughly.
4) Chill at least 30 minutes.
5) Roll out crust and place in pie dish.
6) *Bake in conventional oven at 425°F 8-12 minutes until golden.*

My cooking time _____

Apple Upside-Down Cake  Serves 8–10

2 tart red apples	⅓ cup chopped maraschino cherries
¼ cup butter or margarine	
½ cup honey	1 pkg. spice cake mix
½ cup chopped nuts (optional)	

Continued on next page 113

1) Core unpeeled apples and slice in rings ¼" thick.
2) Melt butter in 10" glass baking dish on High power 45-60 seconds.
3) Add honey and apple rings to butter. Micro-cook on High power 3 minutes.
4) Sprinkle with nuts and fill apple slice centers with cherries.
5) Prepare spice cake batter according to directions on package.
6) Pour 3 cups of batter over apples. Spread evenly.
7) Micro-cook on High power 12-13 minutes until toothpick comes out clean. Rotate dish every 3 minutes.
8) Allow to after-cook 5 minutes. Invert onto serving dish. Serve with ice cream or warm whipped cream.

Tip: Remaining batter may be baked as cupcakes.

My cooking time _____

Ginger-Apple Cake

Serves 6–8

1 14½ oz. pkg. gingerbread mix
2   cups grated apples

1) Mix cake as directed on the package but use only ½ cup of water. Blend in the apples.
2) Spread mixture evenly in a 9" round dish.

Topping

⅓ **cup brown sugar**   ⅓ **cup butter**
⅓ **cup nuts**   ½ **teaspoon cinnamon**

3) Blend all ingredients together and spread on top of cake.
4) Micro-cook on 70% power 8-10 minutes until a toothpick comes out clean. Turn dish twice.
5) Allow to after-cook 10-15 minutes. Serve warm.

My cooking time _____

Beat and Bake Cake

🐞🐞 Serves 6–8

Cake

1	pkg. yellow cake mix	1	8¼ oz. can crushed
2	eggs		pineapple, including juice
½	cup water		

1) Beat all ingredients in a large mixing bowl one minute on slow speed, then 2 minutes on faster setting. Scrape sides of bowl occasionally.
2) Grease the outside of a cheese or jelly glass and push it down into center of mixture, open end up.
3) Micro-cook on 30% power 9 minutes then on High power 5 minutes.
4) Allow to after-cook 10 minutes. Remove glass and invert cake on serving dish. Cover with glacé.

Glacé

1	tablespoon cornstarch	1	tablespoon butter
¼	cup sugar	1	14 oz. can cranberry-orange
⅛	teaspoon salt		relish
½	cup water		

5) Mix all ingredients except relish in a 4-cup glass measure.
6) Micro-cook on High power 2 minutes, stirring 3 times. Mixture will become thick.
7) Add relish. Stir, then chill. Serve with or on cake.

My cooking time _____

Bundt Cake

Packaged Bundt cake

(A full package will require a 12-cup dish, which can be found at import stores, discount and department stores. Smaller bundt dishes may be found that will take half a package.)

1) Grease ceramic dish very well. (If microwave plastic dish is used, grease lightly.) Prepare cake mixture as directed on the package and place in greased dish.
2) Micro-cook on High power 10-12 minutes. Rotate dish one-fourth turn every 3 minutes.
3) Allow to after-cook 10 minutes. Frost or glaze.

Tip: Two flavors that are especially good when micro-cooked are chocolate streusel and chocolate macaroon. Both have eye appeal and a nice texture.

My cooking time ＿＿＿＿＿＿＿＿＿

Easy Carrot-Pineapple Cake with Cream Cheese Frosting

Serves 8–10

Cake

1½ cups all-purpose flour	2 eggs
1 cup sugar	1 cup carrots, shredded fine
1 teaspoon baking powder	½ cup crushed pineapple, with syrup
1 teaspoon cinnamon	
½ teaspoon salt	1 teaspoon vanilla extract
⅔ cup salad oil	

1) Sift flour, sugar, baking powder, cinnamon and salt together, then add remaining ingredients. Beat in a mixer until all ingredients are moistened. (Use medium speed for about 2 minutes.)
2) Pour batter into ungreased 9″ × 9″ × 2″ dish or a 9″ round dish. Spread evenly.
3) Micro-cook on High power 8-8½ minutes until toothpick comes out clean. Rotate dish 2-3 times. Let cool.

Cream Cheese Frosting

3	oz. cream cheese	2½	cups powdered sugar, sifted
4	tablespoons margarine	½	cup chopped pecans
1	teaspoon vanilla extract		(optional)
	dash of salt		

4) Soften cream cheese and margarine in a 4-cup glass measure on High power 45-60 seconds.
5) Add vanilla extract and salt. Beat in powdered sugar. Blend well.
6) Spread frosting over cake. Decorate with nuts. Serve warm or cold.

My cooking time _____

Pound Cake

Serves 10–12

2½	sticks butter	1	tablespoon orange rind
1½	cups sugar		(1 orange)
5	eggs	2	tablespoons orange juice
1	tablespoon lemon rind	¼	teaspoon salt
	(2 lemons)	2½	cups flour

1) Place butter in small glass container and soften on High power 2 minutes.
2) Beat butter and sugar together well, until fluffy.
3) Add eggs, one at a time, beating after each addition.
4) Pour into lightly greased 12-cup bundt cake dish.
5) Micro-cook on High power 4 minutes, then on 70% power 5-6 minutes more or until a toothpick comes out clean. Rotate dish 3 times.
6) Allow to after-cook 10 minutes, then invert onto serving dish.
7) Serve with raspberry sauce (See SAUCES) and poached pears (See DESSERTS).

Tip: Cake is even more delicious when stored two or three days, covered tightly.

My cooking time _____

Chilled Pineapple Pudding Cake ⏱ Serves 6–8

2 tablespoons water	1 cup powdered sugar
4 tablespoons sugar	½ cup crushed pineapple
2 eggs, separated	2 cups crushed vanilla wafers
½ cup butter	

1) Place sugar and water in 4-cup glass measure. Dissolve sugar on High power 45-60 seconds. Stir.
2) Add egg yolks, slightly beaten. Micro-cook on High power 30 seconds. Whip with wire whisk or fork. Micro-cook on High power 15-30 seconds more until mixture is thick and creamy.
3) Place butter in small glass container and soften on High power 30-45 seconds. Cream butter and powdered sugar, then stir into egg mixture. Add crushed pineapple.
4) Beat egg whites until stiff then fold into pineapple mixture.
5) Spread ⅓ of wafer crumbs in a 6″ × 10″ glass dish, cover with half of pineapple mixture. Layer another ⅓ of crumbs then the remaining pineapple mixture. Cover with remaining crumbs.
6) Refrigerate over-night or 8-12 hours.

My cooking time _____

Chocolate Potato Cake ⏱⏱ Serves 12–15

1 cup shortening	1 teaspoon cinnamon
2 cups sugar	2 teaspoons baking powder
4 eggs, separated	½ teaspoon salt
½ cup instant cocoa	½ cup milk
1 cup mashed potatoes	⅛ teaspoon salt
1½ cups flour	

1) Cream shortening with sugar until light and fluffy.
2) Beat in egg yolks, one at a time. Add cocoa and mashed potatoes, mixing until smooth.

3) Sift flour with cinnamon, baking powder and ½ teaspoon salt. Add dry ingredients to shortening mixture, alternating with milk. Mix batter well after each addition.
4) Beat egg whites with ⅛ teaspoon salt until stiff but not dry. Carefully fold egg whites into batter.
5) Pour into slightly greased 12-cup microwave bundt cake dish. Micro-cook on High power 11-13 minutes until toothpick comes out clean. Rotate dish one-fourth turn 3 times while cooking.
6) Allow to after-cook 10 minutes. Loosen edges and turn out on a dish to cool. Sprinkle with powdered sugar.

Tip: Instant mashed potatoes are made easily in the microwave oven. Make according to package directions for 2 servings. Use a 4-cup glass measure and bring liquid to a boil on High power 3-4 minutes. Beat in the potatoes with butter until very smooth. Makes 1 cup.

My cooking time _____

Chocolate Pudding Cake
Serves 6

Cake

¾	cup flour	¼	cup nuts, chopped fine
¼	cup instant cocoa		(optional)
¼	cup sugar	½	cup milk
2	teaspoons baking powder	1	teaspoon vanilla
¼	teaspoon salt	4	tablespoons butter

1) In a 2-quart baking dish, sift flour and mix in cocoa, sugar, baking powder and salt. Stir in nuts.
2) Melt butter in a custard cup on High power 45-60 seconds.
3) Mix milk, vanilla and butter in a small container then stir them into dry ingredients. Blend well. Set aside.

Pudding

¼	cup cocoa mix	¼	teaspoon salt
¼	cup sugar	1	cup boiling water
¼	cup brown sugar, packed		

Continued on next page   119

4) In a 4-cup measure mix chocolate, sugars and salt with boiling water.
5) Pour over cake batter. *Do not stir.*
6) Micro-cook on 70% power 6-7 minutes until toothpick comes out clean. Rotate dish once.
7) Allow to after-cook 20-30 minutes. Serve warm or cold with whipped cream.

My cooking time _____

Chocolate Spice Cake

Serves 6–8

1	cup instant cocoa	½	cup butter or margarine
1½	cups flour	¾	cup milk
1	cup sugar	1½	teaspoon vanilla
1½	teaspoons baking powder	2	eggs
½	teaspoon salt		

1) In a large mixing bowl sift together cocoa, flour, sugar, baking powder and salt.
2) Place butter in small glass container and soften on High power 12-15 seconds.
3) Make a well in center of cocoa-flour mixture and add butter, milk and vanilla. Mix slowly to blend then beat on high speed for 5 minutes.
4) Add eggs one at a time, beating well after each addition.
5) Pour into a greased 1-quart baking dish. Micro-cook on 70% power 8-10 minutes. Rotate dish 3 times.
6) Allow to after-cook 15-20 minutes before slicing. Serve plain or frosted (See MILK CHOCOLATE FROSTING recipe).

My cooking time _____

In-The-Bowl Chocolate Cake  Serves 6–10

1⅓ cups cake flour	1 teaspoon vanilla
1¾ teaspoons baking powder	2 squares baking chocolate,
¼ teaspoon salt	unsweetened
1 cup sugar	5 tablespoons butter or
2 eggs	margarine
½ cup milk	

1) Mix cake flour, baking powder, salt and sugar in a large glass mixing bowl that has been sprayed with Pam or greased lightly.
2) Add eggs, milk and vanilla to mixture. Beat.
3) Place chocolate and butter in small glass container and melt on High power 1-2 minutes.
4) Add chocolate-butter mixture to other ingredients. Beat vigorously 60 seconds until creamy and smooth.
5) Micro-cook on High power 5-7 minutes until toothpick comes out clean. Rotate bowl twice.
6) Allow to after-cook 10 minutes. Cover with Dark Chocolate Sauce (See SAUCES).

My cooking time _____

Quick Apple Coffeecake 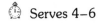 Serves 4–6

Topping

2 tablespoons butter or	1 baking apple (Pippin,
margarine	Gravenstein or Rome
¼ cup brown sugar	Beauty) shredded in food
¼ teaspoon cinnamon	processor or grated

1) Place butter in 8″ round baking dish and melt on High power 20-30 seconds.
2) Tip dish to spread butter evenly then sprinkle brown sugar and cinnamon over butter.

Continued on next page   121

3) Spread shredded apple over brown sugar.
4) Micro-cook on High power 3 minutes. Set dish aside.

Cake

2	cups biscuit mix	1	egg
¼	cup sugar	3	tablespoons cooking oil
1	teaspoon cinnamon	⅔	cup milk

5) In medium size mixing bowl add biscuit mix, sugar and cinnamon. Mix well. Add cooking oil, egg and milk. Stir until well blended.
6) Pour evenly over apple mixture and spread with a spatula. Cover with a paper towel.
7) Micro-cook on 70% power 5-6 minutes or until toothpick comes out clean.
8) Allow to after-cook 5 minutes.
9) Invert onto serving plate. Serve warm with whipped cream.

Tip: When making topping, sprinkle shredded apple with lemon juice to keep apple from turning brown.

My cooking time _____

Graham Streusel Coffeecake 🕐🕐 16 servings

½	cup butter or margarine	¾	teaspoon cinnamon
1	cup graham cracker crumbs (18-20 crackers)	1	18½ oz. pkg. yellow cake mix
⅓	cup nuts, chopped (optional)	1	cup water
½	cup brown sugar, firmly packed	¼	cup vegetable oil
		3	eggs

1) Melt butter in a medium size bowl on High power 60-75 seconds.
2) Add graham cracker crumbs, nuts, brown sugar and cinnamon. Mix well.
3) Grease two 9″ round cake dishes and line with wax paper. Spread one half of crumb mixture into each dish. Set aside.

4) In a large bowl, blend cake mix, water, oil and eggs at medium speed for 3½ minutes. Scrape bowl frequently. Divide one half of batter between the two dishes. Sprinkle one half the crumb mixture over the batter. Repeat with the remaining batter and crumb mixture.
5) Micro-cook on High power 6-8 minutes until toothpick comes out clean.
6) Allow to after-cook 10 minutes, then invert onto serving plate. Remove wax paper and drizzle vanilla glaze over cake.

Vanilla Glaze

1 cup powdered sugar
milk

7) Combine sugar with 1 to 2 tablespoons of milk until desired consistency is reached. Drizzle over cake.

My cooking time _____

Lemon Spice Coffeecake

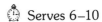 Serves 6–10

Crumb Topping

2 tablespoons butter	⅛ teaspoon salt
⅓ cup brown sugar, firmly packed	¼ cup chopped walnuts
3 tablespoons flour	1 teaspoon grated lemon rind
¼ teaspoon cinnamon	3-4 tablespoons honey wheat germ (optional)

1) Melt butter in 2-quart measure on High power 20-30 seconds.
2) Add remaining ingredients to butter and combine with a fork until crumbly. Set container aside.

Continued on next page

Cake

⅓	cup butter or margarine	¼	teaspoon cinnamon
¾	cup sugar	½	cup buttermilk or sour milk
1	egg	½	cup raisins
1½	cups flour	1	teaspoon grated lemon rind
1½	teaspoon baking powder	¼	cup chopped walnuts
½	teaspoon soda		(optional)
¼	teaspoon nutmeg		

3) Cream butter and sugar together then beat in egg.
4) Sift flour, baking powder, soda, nutmeg and cinnamon together and add to creamed mixture.
5) Fold in buttermilk, raisins, lemon rind and nuts.
6) Spread cake mixture into 6" × 10" dish (9" round dish) and sprinkle topping evenly over the top.
7) Micro-cook on 70% power 6-7 minutes or until toothpick comes out clean. Rotate dish once or twice.

Tip: ½ cup milk may be soured by adding 1 teaspoon vinegar or lemon juice.

My cooking time _____

Orange Streusel Coffeecake   🕐 Serves 4–6

Cake

1 pkg. orange muffin mix
4-5 tablespoons apricot jam

1) Prepare muffin mix in accordance with directions on box.
2) Place mixture in 8" round cake dish. Dot with jam. Set dish aside.

Topping

3	tablespoons flour	1-2	teaspoons cinnamon
3	tablespoons sugar	2	tablespoons butter (firm)

3) Blend flour, sugar and cinnamon together in 4-cup measure.
4) Cut in butter until mixture is crumbly.
5) Spread topping over streusel cake mixture.
6) Micro-cook on High power 5-7 minutes. Rotate dish every 2 minutes.

Tip: Try pineapple muffin mix too.

My cooking time _____

Strawberry Cake

 Serves 12

1 large pkg. white cake mix	½ cup frozen strawberries
1 pkg. strawberry Jello	defrosted, juice and all
⅔ cup Wesson oil	4 eggs
½ cup water	

1) Mix all ingredients in large mixing bowl. Beat well.
2) Pour mixture into lightly greased (shortening works best) 12-cup bundt cake dish.
3) Micro-cook on High power 11-13 minutes. Rotate dish 3 times.
4) Allow to after-cook 7-10 minutes. Loosen edge with knife and unmold onto serving dish.
5) Drizzle pink glaze over cake.

Pink Glaze

2 cups Confectioner's sugar	red food coloring (1 drop)
¼ cup milk	

6) Mix ingredients thoroughly, adding milk slowly until glaze is thick enough to pour like heavy cream.

My cooking time _____

Spicy Pumpkin Squares

Makes 2 dozen

½ cup butter or margarine
1 cup brown sugar, firmly packed
1 egg
½ cup canned pumpkin
1½ cups all-purpose flour, unsifted

1 teaspoon cinnamon
½ teaspoon ginger
½ teaspoon allspice
½ teaspoon baking soda
½ cup raisins or chopped dates
½ cup chopped walnuts or pecans

1) Place butter in large mixing bowl and soften on high power 30-45 seconds. Cream brown sugar and butter until fluffy.
2) Beat in egg and pumpkin until well combined. (Mixture will look curdled or separated.)
3) Sift flour with spices and baking soda. Carefully blend flour mixture into creamed mixture. Stir in raisins and nuts.
4) Spread batter evenly in ungreased 2-quart utility dish. Micro-cook on 70% power 8-9 minutes. Rotate 2 times.
5) When done, batter will pull away from sides of dish and center will test almost done when toothpick is inserted.
6) Place cake on rack until almost cool, then lightly spread on Orange Icing. When icing is set, cut into squares.

Orange Icing

1 cup powdered sugar, unsifted
4 teaspoons defrosted frozen orange concentrate

2 teaspoons milk or light cream

7) Blend all ingredients together until smooth.

My cooking time _____

Instant Jello Cake

Serves 4–6

1 7½ oz. jar pear and pineapple Junior baby food

1 pkg. strawberry or lime Jello
1 9 oz. yellow cake mix

1) Mix baby food and Jello and spread in a 9″ round glass dish.
2) Prepare cake mix according to directions on package and pour evenly over top of Jello-fruit mixture.
3) Micro-cook on 70% power 6-7 minutes until a toothpick comes out clean.
4) Allow to after-cook 10 minutes then invert onto a serving dish. Dust with powdered sugar, if desired.

Tip: Super easy for children to make.

My cooking time _____

Grandma's Apple Crisp

Serves 6–8

6 medium apples, Pippin or Gravenstein, peeled and sliced thin	⅔ cup rolled oats
	½ teaspoon nutmeg
	¾ teaspoon cinnamon
¾ cup brown sugar	½ cup butter
½ cup flour	

1) Layer apples evenly in 9″ round baking dish.
2) Using a pastry blender, blend all other ingredients together until mixture becomes crumbly. Spread mixture evenly over top of apples.
3) Micro-cook on High power 6-8 minutes. Rotate dish half way through cooking time. When done, apples should be soft.

My cooking time _____

Baked Apples

Prepare one apple per person

apples	cinnamon	butter
sugar	raisins	

Continued on next page   127

1) Core apples and fill with sugar, cinnamon, raisins and a little butter. Place apples in a covered container.
2) Micro-cook on High power 3-4½ minutes.
3) Allow to after-cook a few minutes before serving.

My cooking time _____

Grapefruit Royale

 One-half grapefruit per person

Sprinkle each half of grapefruit with one teaspoon brown sugar. Heat on High power 30 seconds.

My cooking time _____

Poached Pears

🕐 Serves 4–6

4-6	medium pears	peel of one orange
1	teaspoon vanilla extract	1	cup sugar
	peel of one lemon		water

1) Peel pears. Start at bottom and work upwards with peeler. Leave stem. Wrap each pear in a wet paper towel to keep from turning brown. Set aside.
2) Add remaining ingredients to a 3-quart casserole dish. Use enough water to cover pears to the stem. (Pears are placed in syrup in step 4.).
3) Bring mixture to a boil on High power 5-8 minutes. Mixture will become a syrup. Stir.
4) Remove wet paper towels and place pears in syrup, standing up. Lay a wet paper towel on top of pears and cover dish with lid or plastic film.
5) Micro-cook on High power 8-10 minutes until fork tender.

My cooking time _____

Peanut Brittle Pumpkin Custard ⏲⏲ Serves 10–12

2 eggs, slightly beaten	½ teaspoon ginger
1½ cups solid pack pumpkin	¼ teaspoon ground cloves
(½ of 29 oz. can)	1 13 fl. oz. can evaporated milk
¾ cup sugar	½ lb. small pieces peanut
½ teaspoon salt	brittle
1 teaspoon cinnamon	10-12 6 oz. custard cups

1) Mix ingredients, except peanut brittle, in order given in a large mixing bowl.
2) Fill custard cups ⅔ full of mixture and sprinkle 1 tablespoon of peanut brittle on each. Place 5-6 cups in circular pattern in microwave oven. Leave space between cups.
3) Micro-cook on 70% power 3 minutes. Rotate each cup, then micro-cook on 70% power 4-5 minutes more. Mixture should look like almost molded Jello.
4) Allow to after-cook 15-20 minutes to thicken. Refrigerate.
5) Repeat for remaining cups.

My cooking time _____

Easy Pudding

⏲ Serves 4–6

1 3¼ oz. pkg. pudding
milk as required by pudding directions

1) Place contents of pudding package in medium mixing bowl.
2) Add milk according to pudding directions. Stir.
3) Let mixture stand for a few seconds, then micro-cook on High power 2½ minutes.
4) Stir and micro-cook on High power 3½ minutes more.
5) Cover bowl lightly and allow to cool. Stir once or twice while cooling. Serve warm or refrigerate until cold.

My cooking time _____

Peach Pie

1 pre-baked 9″ pie crust (See ALL PURPOSE PIE CRUST recipe)

1	teaspoon unflavored gelatin	½	cup whipping crean
2	tablespoons cold water	3	tablespoons cream sherry
1	12 oz. jar (1 cup) apricot preserves	¼	teaspoon cinnamon maraschino cherries
1	2 lb. 13 oz. can peach halves, drained		

1) Combine gelatin and cold water in a container.
2) Place apricot preserves in a dish and micro-cook to boiling on High power 2-3 minutes.
3) Add gelatin mixture to preserves and stir to dissolve gelatin.
4) Add sherry and stir.
5) Allow to cool until mixture becomes slighly thickened.
6) Place peach halves (hollow side down) on baked pie crust. Spoon preserve mixture over peaches. Chill.
7) Serve with whipped cream spread over the pie and garnish with maraschino cherries.

My cooking time _____

Chocolate Mint Pie Freeze

Serves 6–8

Graham Cracker Crust

18-20	Graham crackers
¼	cup butter
2	tablespoons sugar

1) Crush Graham crackers finely in blender. Add sugar and blend.
2) Melt butter in 9″ pie plate on High power 45-60 seconds.
3) Mix in crushed crackers and spread over entire pie plate. Press with fingers to mold into place.

4) Micro-cook on High power 2-2½ minutes. Rotate dish after 1½ minutes. Set aside to cool.

Filling

1 pint mint chocolate chip ice cream

5) Soften ice cream in its container on High power 30 seconds.
6) Spoon ice cream into crust. Freeze the pie.

Topping

2 (2 oz.) squares baking chocolate	**1 tablespoon butter**
½ cup sugar	**1 13 oz. can evaporated milk**

7) Melt chocolate and butter on 70% power 1½-2 minutes in a 4 cup glass measure. Stir.
8) Add evaporated milk and sugar. Blend well.
9) Micro-cook on High power 2-2½ minutes more until topping is thick and smooth. Stir often.
10) Allow to cool 1 hour, then spread over ice cream. Freeze until serving time.

My cooking time _____

Milk Chocolate Frosting

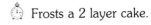 Frosts a 2 layer cake.

1 10 oz. pkg. milk chocolate squares	**¼ cup milk**
1 teaspoon butter	**1 teaspoon vanilla**
	dash of salt

1) Place chocolate and butter in a 1-quart measure. Melt on 70% power 4–6 minutes. Stir twice while melting.
2) Allow to after-cook 2-3 minutes. Stir in milk and salt.
3) Add vanilla and beat until thick and smooth. Cool slightly, then frost cake or cupcakes.

My cooking time _____

Cherry Jewel Divinity

😊😊 Makes 25–30 pieces

2 cups sugar	½ cup nuts, chopped fine
½ cup light Karo syrup	1 teaspoon vanilla
⅓ cup water	¾ cup candied cherries,
2 egg whites	chopped fine

1) Combine sugar, syrup and water in a 3-quart bowl.
2) Micro-cook on High power 5 minutes or until liquid is clear. Stir vigorously, then micro-cook on High power 7-8 minutes more. (Syrup is ready when a small amount will form a hard crystal-like ball when dropped into very cold water. 260° on candy thermometer.)
3) While syrup is cooking, beat egg whites until stiff peaks form.
4) When syrup is ready, beat egg whites while *slowly* pouring in a thin stream of the hot syrup.
5) Add vanilla and beat until the candy mixture loses its gloss. This takes about 6-8 minutes.
6) Stir in nuts and cherries.
7) Drop the candy mixture onto wax paper by the spoonful or spread into a 2-quart baking dish.
8) Allow to cool. If glass dish is used, cut candy into squares.

Tip: Divinity should be made when humidity is low.

My cooking time _____

Cherry Crunch Dessert

😊😊 Serves 6

1½ cups sifted all-purpose flour	½ teaspoon soda
¾ cup quick-cooking rolled oats	½ teaspoon salt
1 cup firmly packed brown sugar	½ cup butter
	1 (1 lb. 3 oz.) can prepared cherry pie filling

1) Place butter in small glass container and soften on High power 15-20 seconds.

2) Mix dry ingredients in a large mixing bowl. Cut in butter and mix well until particles of mixture are small and uniform.
3) Pat half of mixture into a 9″ square baking dish.
4) Cover crumb layer evenly with pie filling. Sprinkle remaining mixture over filling.
5) Micro-cook on High power 14-16 minutes. Turn dish every 5 minutes.
6) Serve warm or cold.

My cooking time _____

Fabulous Fudge

 Makes 25–35 pieces

¾ cup evaporated milk	1 12 oz. pkg. chocolate chips
1 tablespoon butter or margarine	1 cup chopped nuts
1½ cups sugar	1 teaspoon vanilla
2 cups miniature marshmallows	

1) Combine milk, butter, sugar and marshmallows in a 2-quart bowl.
2) Micro-cook on High power 3-4 minutes until mixture begins to boil.
3) Stir mixture and reduce to 70% power 3-4 minutes more until mixture boils again and sugar completely dissolves.
4) Stir in chocolate chips, nuts and vanilla. Beat until smooth.
5) Spread mixture in an 8″ × 8″ dish. Let cool then cut into 1″ squares.

My cooking time _____

Black Bean Sauce For Fish

3	tablespoons black beans, well rinsed	2	teaspoons sesame oil or peanut oil
2	cloves garlic, crushed		dash of Accent
3	tablespoons soy sauce		

1) Mash beans well in 1-quart measure.
2) Add remaining ingredients. Stir to blend. Brush on fish.

My cooking time _____

Bourbon Glaze for Ham   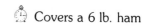 Covers a 6 lb. ham

1	cup brown sugar	1	teaspoon dry mustard
3	tablespoons flour	4	tablespoons bourbon

1) Mix brown sugar, flour and mustard with a fork in a 2-quart measure.
2) Stir in bourbon. Use additional bourbon if glaze is too thick.
3) Micro-cook on High power 45-75 seconds.
4) Spread on ham at half-way point of ham cooking time.

Tip: Rum makes a delicious substitute for the bourbon in this recipe.

My cooking time _____

Cranberry

🕐 Serves 8–10

1	**lb. fresh cranberries (or 1 16 oz. pkg.)**
1¼	**cups sugar**
1	**cup red currant preserves**
½	**cup orange juice**

1	**cup walnuts, chopped fine (optional)**
2	**tablespoons orange peel, grated**

1) Combine cranberries, sugar, preserves and orange juice in a large bowl. Bring to a boil on High power 3-4 minutes. Stir.
2) Micro-cook on 70% power 8-10 minutes. Stir twice. Skim off foam.
3) Add nuts and orange peel. Stir. Refrigerate at least 6 hours.

My cooking time _____

Dark Chocolate

🕐 Serves 4–6

½	**cup sugar**
3½	**tablespoons cocoa**
1½	**tablespoons cornstarch**
½	**cup water**

2	**tablespoons butter or margarine**
1	**teaspoon vanilla**
	dash of salt

1) Mix dry ingredients in a 2-cup measure. Stir in water.
2) Micro-cook on High power 2 minutes, stirring twice.
3) Add butter and micro-cook on High power 1 minute more.
4) Stir well. Blend in vanilla.

My cooking time _____

Super Chocolate

1⅓ cups instant cocoa   1 cup hot water
1 cup sugar   1 teaspoon vanilla
⅛ teaspoon salt

1) Combine cocoa, sugar and salt in a 1½-quart dish.
2) Add hot water and stir until cocoa is dissolved.
3) Micro-cook on High power 3-4 minutes until mixture comes to a boil. Reduce to 50% power and micro-cook 60-90 seconds more.
4) Stir in vanilla. Allow to after-cook 5 minutes.
5) Serve hot or cold over ice cream, cake or pudding.

My cooking time _____

Hollandaise Sauce-I

¼ cup butter or margarine   2 tablespoons evaporated milk
2 teaspoons lemon juice   ⅛ teaspoon salt
2 egg yolks, beaten well

1) Melt butter in 2-cup measure on High power 45-60 seconds.
2) Stir in lemon juice, egg yolks and milk. Whip and stir after each is added.
3) Micro-cook on High power 15 seconds. Whip and stir then micro-cook on High power 15 seconds more. Whip and stir until mixture begins to thicken. Micro-cook on High power 15 seconds more. Whip and Stir.
4) Allow sauce to after-cook a few seconds, stir and serve. Delicious over freshly cooked asparagus, cauliflower or broccoli.

Tip: Sauce can be made ahead of time and warmed before serving. Warm on 70% power 20-40 seconds. Stir after 10 seconds.

My cooking time _____

Hollandaise Sauce-II

 Serves 4

1 stick butter	4 egg yolks, slightly beaten
4 teaspoons lemon juice	dash of salt
4 tablespoons evaporated milk	dash of dry mustard

1) Melt butter in 4-cup measure on High power 60-90 seconds.
2) While whipping butter with fork or wire whisk, add remaining ingredients one at a time. Whip after each addition.
3) Micro-cook on High power 60-90 seconds or until sauce is fluffy and thick. *Whip every 20 seconds while cooking.*
4) Allow sauce to after-cook 1 minute.

My cooking time _____

Jiffy Cheese

½ cup sharp Cheddar cheese, shredded	½ cup milk
	½ cup mayonnaise

1) Combine all ingredients in a small mixing bowl.
2) Micro-cook on High power 45 seconds, stir and micro-cook on High power 1½ minutes more until sauce is thick.
3) Cover any left-over sauce with plastic film and refrigerate.
4) To reheat, place container right from the refrigerator into microwave oven. Use 70% power 1-1½ minutes. Stir after 45 seconds. Add a little milk if sauce is thicker than desired.

Tip: Make as much sauce as desired, just keep the proportions equal.

My cooking time _____

Lemon

½ cup sugar
1 tablespoon cornstarch
1 cup water
dash salt

2 tablespoons butter or margarine
2 tablespoons lemon juice
½ teaspoon grated lemon rind

1) Combine sugar and cornstarch in a 4-cup container. Stir in water.
2) Micro-cook on High power 2 minutes. Stir twice.
3) Blend in butter, grated lemon rind, lemon juice and salt.
4) Micro-cook on High power 30-60 seconds more.

Tip: Delicious over gingerbread or spice cake.

My cooking time _____

Mornay

Makes 1½–2 cups

¼ cup butter
¼ cup flour
¾ teaspoon salt
2½ cups milk
2 egg yolks, slightly beaten
2 tablespoons evaporated milk or heavy cream

4 tablespoons Parmesan cheese, grated
1 teaspoon garlic salt
3 tablespoons parsley, chopped
2 tablespoons very dry sherry

1) Place butter in a 4-cup measure and melt on High power 45-60 seconds.
2) Stir in flour and salt. Blend to a smooth paste.
3) Slowly add milk, then egg yolks, stirring constantly.
4) Micro-cook, uncovered, on High power 1½ minutes. Stir well.
5) Add remaining ingredients, except parsley. Stir well until blended.
6) Micro-cook on High power 1 minute. Stir and micro-cook on High power 1-2 minutes more until sauce is of consistency of heavy cream.
7) Add parsley and serve.

My cooking time _____

Mushroom-Cheese

2	tablespoons butter	½	cup sharp Cheddar cheese, shredded
4	tablespoons flour		
½	teaspoon salt	1	2½ oz. can chopped mushrooms, with liquid
1	cup milk		

1) Place butter in a 4-cup measure and melt on High power 20-30 seconds.
2) Stir in flour and salt. Blend to a smooth paste.
3) Slowly add milk, stirring constantly.
4) Micro-cook on High power 1 minute. Stir and micro-cook on High power 1½ minutes more, stirring every 45 seconds.
5) Add cheese. Micro-cook on 70% power 1-2 minutes, stirring every minute.
6) Add mushrooms and liquid. Stir until blended. Micro-cook on 70% power 1 minute more.
7) Stir and serve. Delicious over cauliflower or green beans.

My cooking time _____

Plum

¼	cup plum jam	3	tablespoons brown sugar
¼	cup currant jelly	2	tablespoons white sugar
2	tablespoons cider vinegar		

1) Mix all ingredients in a 2-quart measure.
2) Micro-cook on High power 60-90 seconds.

Tip: Excellent served with pork chops.

My cooking time _____

Raspberry

Serves 4–6

2 10 oz. pkgs. frozen raspberries
2 tablespoons red raspberry preserves

1) Puncture each package of raspberries with a fork and defrost on High power 2-2½ minutes.
2) Mix raspberries and preserves in blender.
3) Strain mixture and place in a 4-cup measure.
4) Micro-cook on High power 5-8 minutes. Mixture should boil for 3 minutes. Strain again.
5) Cool mixture in refrigerator and serve on ice cream, poached pears or cake.

My cooking time _____

White

2	**tablespoons butter or margarine**	**½**	**teaspoon salt**
2	**tablespoons flour**	**1**	**cup milk**
			dash of nutmeg

1) Place butter in a 2-cup measure and melt on High power 20-30 seconds.
2) Stir in flour and salt until smooth, then add milk gradually while continuing to stir. Add nutmeg.
3) Micro-cook on High power 1 minute. Stir well and micro-cook on High power 1½-2 minutes more. Stir every 30 seconds.

My cooking time _____

Zippy Fruit Bake

2	cups canned peaches, drained	4	tablespoons margarine
2	cups canned apricots, drained	4	tablespoons brown sugar
1	cup frozen ollalie berries or canned crushed pineapple	3	tablespoons curry powder slivered almonds

1) Mix all ingredients except almonds in a 4-quart measure and micro-cook on High power 3 minutes. Stir and micro-cook on High power 3 minutes more.
2) Top with almonds and serve.

Tip: Great with pork roast of ribs.

My cooking time _____

Chocolate Banana

Makes 1 loaf

½ cup butter or margarine
⅓ cup sugar
2 eggs
1 cup instant cocoa
1½ cups bananas, mashed

½ cup walnuts, chopped
    (optional)
1¾ cups flour
1 teaspoon baking soda
1 teaspoon baking powder
½ teaspoon salt

1) In large mixing bowl cream butter lightly with sugar. Mix in eggs, one at a time. Add cocoa and beat until smooth.
2) Mix in bananas and walnuts.
3) Sift flour with baking powder, baking soda and salt. Mixing by hand, add dry ingredients all at one time. Do not over-mix.
4) Pour into 1-quart tube dish. Micro-cook on 70% power 8-10 minutes. Rotate dish twice.
5) Allow to after-cook 5 minutes. Loosen edges and unmold onto a rack to cool.

My cooking time _____

Chocolate Chip Pumpkin  Makes 2 loaves

Bread

4	eggs	¾	teaspoon nutmeg
3	cups sugar	1½	teaspoons cinnamon
1	cup oil	¾	teaspoon allspice
2	cups canned pumpkin	½	teaspoon ginger
3	cups flour	⅔	cup water
2	teaspoons baking soda	½	cup walnuts, chopped
2	teaspoons salt		(optional)
1	teaspoon baking powder	1	6 oz. pkg. chocolate chips

1) In large mixing bowl combine eggs, sugar, oil. Cream together, using electric mixer on high speed for 5 minutes. On medium speed blend in pumpkin.
2) Sift flour with baking soda, salt, baking powder and spices. Add dry ingredients alternately with water. (Begin and end with dry ingredients.)
3) Mix until smooth, but do not over-beat.
4) Fold in nuts and chocolate chips.
5) Lightly grease two 1½-quart tube dishes. Spread batter into the two dishes.
6) Micro-cook dishes one at a time on 70% power 18-20 minutes until toothpick comes out clean. Rotate dish several times. Repeat for second dish.
7) Allow loaves to cool outside of microwave oven.

Spicy Glaze

½	cup powdered sugar	1	tablespoon salt
⅛	teaspoon nutmeg		milk
¼	teaspoon cinnamon		

8) In a small mixing bowl mix all ingredients with a fork or wire whisk. Add milk to obtain consistency desired. Drizzle glaze over loaves.

My cooking time _____

143

Garlic 'N Chives San Francisco Sour Dough

1	1 lb. loaf sour dough bread	1	clove fresh garlic, crushed
1	teaspoon fresh or dry chopped chives	½	cup butter (1 stick)

1) Place butter in 2-cup glass measure and soften on High power 12 seconds. Mix chives and garlic into butter.
2) Split bread loaf lengthwise. Spread each half of loaf with butter mixture. Cut 2″ slits across each half. Place loaf back together and cut in half across width. Wrap each half in plastic film.
3) When ready to heat, place each half in a brown bag. Splash a little water in bag just before heating. Heat on High power 30 seconds. It is best to heat each half just before it is served.

Tip: Heating bread in the microwave oven is tricky. Think in seconds.

My cooking time _____

Hot Spice Cider

 Serves 8–10

2   quarts cider
2   cinnamon sticks
1½ cups orange juice
1   tablespoon brown sugar
1   sliced lemon

1   whole orange studded with cloves (stick cloves into orange until it resembles a porcupine)

1) Mix all ingredients except lemon and orange in a punch bowl.
2) Place orange on a paper plate and micro-cook on High power 6-7 minutes. Set aside.
3) Micro-cook cider on High power 20 minutes. Stir 2-3 times while cooking.
4) Add lemon slices and orange. Serve while warm.

My cooking time _____

Hot Butter-Spiced Brandy

 Serves 8 (7 oz. each)

1   qt. apple cider
½ cup lemon juice
⅓ cup honey
½ teaspoon pumpkin pie spice

2   cups brandy
4   teaspoons butter
8   cinnamon sticks

Continued on next page   145

1) Combine cider, lemon juice, honey and pumpkin pie spice in a large measure. Bring to a boil on High power 5-7 minutes.
2) Divide brandy among 8 mugs. Add ½ cup of cider mixture to each mug. Top with ½ teaspoon butter per mug and garnish with cinnamon stick.

My cooking time _____

Flaming Archbishop

⏱ Serves 8

peel of 2 oranges   **1   fifth tawny port**
20   cloves   **1   pint brandy**

1) Stud orange peels with cloves at 1-inch intervals. Place orange peels and port in glass punch bowl.
2) Bring port to a boil on High power 4-5 minutes. Stir in brandy. Ignite punch. Let burn 15 seconds for visual effect. Serve in cups.

My cooking time _____

Microwave Party Chocolate

⏱⏱ Serves 25

1 lb. can instant cocoa
1 gallon milk

1) Place milk in glass punch bowl and heat on High power 18-20 minutes until hot.
2) Stir in cocoa and blend with wire whisk until well mixed.
3) Serve hot.

My cooking time _____

Old Swedish Glögg

½ cup dark raisins
2 prunes
2 cinnamon sticks
5 cardamom seeds
2 cloves
peel of 1 orange

1 cup water
2 fifths tawny port
1¼ cups brandy
½ cup rum
¼ cup sugar

1) Place raisins, prunes, cinnamon, cardamom, cloves, orange peel and water in a large measure. Heat to boiling on High power 2-3 minutes. When boiling, reduce to 50% power 5-6 minutes.
2) While fruit mixture is cooking, warm a glass punch bowl by pouring 2 cups of hot tap water into bowl.
3) Pour water from bowl and transfer fruit mixture to punch bowl.
4) Combine port, brandy, rum and sugar into fruit mixture. Stir continuously.
5) Heat punch on High power 2-3 minutes. Do not boil.
6) Ignite punch. Let burn 15 seconds for visual effect. Serve.

My cooking time _____

Swedish Glögg àu Chocolat

Serves 12

1 fifth burgundy wine
1 fifth ruby port wine
½ cup raisins
¼ cup whole almonds
¼ cup sugar
2 tablespoons instant cocoa
2 cinnamon sticks

1 tablespoon orange marmalade
10 whole cloves
10 cardamom seeds
2 tablespoons brandy
dash of Angostura bitters

1) In a large glass punch bowl, combine burgundy, port, raisins, almonds, sugar, cocoa, cinnamon and marmalade.
2) Put cloves and cardamom seeds into a plastic tea holder or garni bag and place in wine mixture. Cover bowl with wax paper.

Continued on next page 147

3) Micro-heat on 70% power 6-7 minutes or until hot. Stir twice while heating.
4) Add bitters and brandy. Stir and serve.

Tip: Wine mixture may be made ahead of time. To serve, warm on High power 3-4 minutes, then add bitters and brandy.

My cooking time _____

Eggs Benedict and Hollandaise Sauce

Serves 2

Hollandaise Sauce

¼ cup butter or margarine	2 tablespoons evaporated milk
2 teaspoons lemon juice	⅛ teaspoon salt
2 egg yolks, beaten well	

1) Melt butter in 2-cup measure on High power 45-60 seconds.
2) Stir in lemon juice, egg yolks and milk. Whip and stir after each is added.
3) Micro-cook on High power 15 seconds. Whip and stir, then micro-cook on High power 15 seconds more. Whip and stir until mixture begins to thicken. Micro-cook on High power 15 seconds more. Whip and stir.

148

4) Remove container from microwave oven. Stir mixture until smooth then cover container with plastic film and set aside.

Tip: Sauce can be made ahead of time and warmed before serving. Warm on 70% power 20-40 seconds. Stir after 10 seconds.

Eggs Benedict

2	**English muffins, split**	**4** slices cooked ham or 6
4	**eggs**	slices crisp bacon

5) Poach eggs. (See POACHED EGGS recipe)
6) While eggs are poaching, *toast muffins and butter lightly.*
7) Place muffins on plate, put ham or bacon on muffins then place a poached egg on each muffin. Spoon Hollandaise sauce over all.
8) Micro-heat on High power 30-45 seconds.

My cooking time _____

Jiffy Cheese Omelet

1 **slice favorite cheese, grated,**
for each egg
number of eggs desired

chopped avocado, chopped
tomato or crumbled bacon
to taste

1) Place cheese in bowl large enough to hold eggs. Add eggs and blend with wire whisk or fork. Add other desired ingredients.
2) Micro-cook on 70% power according to schedule below. Allow omelet to after-cook several minutes before serving:

One egg—45-60 seconds. My cooking time: _____

Two eggs—1½-2 minutes. My cooking time: _____

Four eggs—2½-3 minutes. My cooking time: _____

Poached Eggs

2 eggs

1) Use a 1-quart dish with lid. Fill half full with hot tap water. Bring water to a boil on High power.
2) Crack egg shells and slip eggs into boiling water.
3) Carefully puncture each yolk with a toothpick. A little bubble will appear similar to the head of a pin. This assures that the egg will not explode.
4) Micro-cook on 70% power according to schedule below. Allow eggs to after-cook 30-60 seconds before serving:

One egg—45-60 seconds.   My cooking time: _____

Two eggs—1¼-1½ minutes.   My cooking time: _____

Three eggs—1¾2 minutes.   My cooking time: _____

Scrambled Eggs with Bacon Bits

2 eggs per person
2 teaspoons milk or cream per egg
bacon bits

1) Use a bowl large enough to hold eggs. Rub inside of bowl with a butter wrapper or use non-stick spray.
2) Break eggs into bowl. Add milk. Beat with wire whisk or fork to blend. Add bacon bits.
3) Cover bowl with lid or plastic film. Micro-cook on 70% power until eggs look almost done. If cooking 4 or fewer eggs, stir every 60 seconds. If cooking 5 or more eggs, stir every 2½ minutes.
4) Whip again and serve. Remember, eggs will after-cook while being served.

My cooking time _____

Super Sandwiches and Soups

Tip: Don't over-heat or the bread will become leathery and chewy. Think in seconds!

Grilled Cheese

1) *Toast bread in conventional toaster.*
2) Butter bread, add a little mayonnaise and the cheese. Heat on 70% power 25-35 seconds.

My cooking time _____

Ham and Cheese on Rye

Make sandwich your favorite way. Heat on 70% power 25-35 seconds.

Tip: Try butter, mayonnaise and Dijon mustard.

My cooking time _____

Protein Special

Spread one slice of whole wheat bread with one teaspoon mayonnaise and 2 ounces of your favorite cheese. Heat on 70% power 20-25 seconds.

My cooking time _____

Tuna Salad with Cheese

2 hamburger buns	3 tablespoons salad dressing
1 6 oz. can tuna	2 tablespoons green onions,
¼ cup sweet pickle relish	chopped
butter	sharp Cheddar cheese

1) If hamburger buns are frozen, defrost on High power 30 seconds, two buns stacked.
2) Mix tuna, relish, salad dressing and onions in a small bowl.
3) Butter buns, then spread on tuna mixture. Sprinkle with grated sharp Cheddar cheese.
4) Heat open-faced on High power: 2 sandwiches—30 seconds, 4 sandwiches—45-60 seconds

My cooking time _____

Pocket Bread (Pita) Supper

 Serves 4

4 pcs. pocket bread	2 tablespoons green pepper,
¾ lb. lean ground beef	minced
3 green onions, chopped	¾ teaspoon Beau Monde
1 tomato, diced	seasoning

1) Mix all ingredients except bread and tomato in a 1-quart measure. Micro-cook on High power 4-6 minutes.
2) Stir tomato into hot mixture and set aside.
3) Heat bread on High power 20-30 seconds.
4) Slice bread open and fill with hot mixture.

Tip: Shredded lettuce or alfalfa sprouts and chopped pickle add texture and zest.

My cooking time _____

S.B.T. Super Sandwich

1 large sandwich

2 slices favorite bread	3 slices avocado
½ cup roast beef, sliced thin	2 heaping tablespoons alfalfa
1 slice Mozzarella or Monterey	sprouts
Jack cheese, thinly cut	mayonnaise to taste

1) Place roast beef on paper plate or wax paper and heat on High power 25 seconds. Remove from microwave oven and place cheese on paper plate or wax paper and heat on 70% power 20 seconds. Remove from microwave oven.
2) Spread mayonnaise on bread, then add roast beef, cheese and remaining ingredients. Heat on paper plate or wax paper on 70% power 20 seconds.
3) Garnish with pickle or cherry peppers.

My cooking time _____

Broccoli Soup

Serves 12

2 10 oz. pkgs. chopped, frozen broccoli	1 tablespoon flour
	1 teaspoon salt
¼ cup onion, chopped	⅛ teaspoon mace
2 cups chicken broth, boiling	⅛ teaspoon pepper
2 tablespoons butter	2 cups half and half

1) Defrost broccoli by puncturing 2 holes in each box and heating on High power 6 minutes.
2) Chicken broth may be boiled in 4-cup measure on High power 4-5 minutes.

Continued on next page

3) Add broccoli and onion to broth and micro-cook on 50% power 5 minutes. Set aside.
4) Place butter in a 2-cup measure and melt on High power 20-30 seconds. Stir flour into butter until smooth. Add salt, mace and pepper and stir to make a smooth paste.
5) Add paste to hot broth and stir until smooth.
6) Micro-cook on 70% power 3-4 minutes until soup thickens.
7) Pour soup into food processor or blender and blend 5 seconds, using plastic blade.
8) Pour soup into serving bowl and slowly add half and half, stirring continuously. Cover to keep warm or refrigerate if not ready to serve.
9) To serve, heat on 70% power 3-5 minutes. Stir before serving.

My cooking time _____

Canned Soups

Serves 2

1 10½ oz. can of soup

1) Follow directions on can. Mix soup in a bowl and place in microwave oven.
2) Micro-cooking times on High power for various amounts of soups are: 1 can—2½-3½ minutes, 2 cans—4-5 minutes, 1 cup—1-1½ minutes
3) Soup can be reheated right from the refrigerator in 2-2½ minutes.

My cooking time _____

Carrot Soup

🕐 Serves 6–8

2 medium onions, sliced
2 tablespoons butter
2 cups carrots, grated (about 3 carrots)
1 14 oz. can chicken broth

½ teaspoon salt
½ cup instant rice
2 cups milk
⅛ teaspoon white pepper

1) Place onions and butter in 1-quart dish with lid. Cover and micro-cook on High power 2-3 minutes.
2) Add carrots and micro-cook on High power 5-7 minutes more.
3) Add broth and rice and allow container to sit on counter 5 minutes, then micro-cook on High power 3-4 minutes more.
4) Pour half of soup into food processor or blender. Blend for 30 seconds. Pour soup from blender into large glass bowl. Blend remaining half of soup 30 seconds and pour into same glass bowl.
5) Add milk, salt and pepper. Micro-cook on 70% power 3-4 minutes until very hot. Soup will thicken. Stir 2 or 3 times.
6) Garnish with chopped parsley or chives.

My cooking time _____

Clam Chowder

🕐 Serves 6–8

2 6 oz. cans minced clams and juice
1 10 oz. can cream of potato soup
1 cup half and half

1 medium onion, chopped fine (or equal amount of onion flakes)
1 cup homogenized milk
8 pcs. cooked bacon

1) Combine all ingredients except bacon into 3-quart casserole.
2) Salt and pepper to taste. Crumble in bacon.
3) Micro-cook on High power 8-10 minutes. Stir twice.

My cooking time _____

Dilly Tomato Soup

Serves 8

6 cups tomato juice or 3 10½ oz. cans tomato soup
4 tablespoons sugar
½ teaspoon salt
1 teaspoon garlic salt

2 tablespoons Worcestershire sauce
2 dashes tabasco
½ cup dill pickle juice
⅓ cup lemon juice

1) Combine all ingredients in a 2-quart mixing bowl and bring to boil on High power 6-8 minutes.
2) Pour soup into serving bowls.

Garnish

½ cup sour cream
1 teaspoon horseradish

4 tablespoons chopped chives

3) Mix horseradish and sour cream. Place a spoonful on each serving of soup. Sprinkle chives over all.

My cooking time _____

SPECIAL DIET COOKERY

Did you know that every gram of fat we consume has twice as many calories as a gram of carbohydrate or protein? That, if we eat foods that are high in water and fiber content, we will feel full because of the volume of the food and yet we would consume fewer calories?

These are important facts for those needing or wanting to lose weight and reduce the risk of hardening of the arteries (atherosclerosis), which causes heart attack and stroke. Individuals with diabetes also can use these principles to lessen the demand on the body to produce insulin.

The microwave oven can be a tremendous boon to achieving these goals. **The advantages of the microwave oven make it much easier to follow special diets. Why?**

1. **Foods do not dehydrate easily when micro-cooked. Therefore we need no butter to saute foods.**

2. **Foods retain their flavor and nutrients, which precludes the need for heavy seasonings.**

3. **Single servings can be prepared quickly and easily.**

4. **Larger recipes can be prepared at a single time because they will not lose nutritional value or flavor when reheated.**

159

I have included suggested menus and recipes. Ways to utilize your microwave oven to the optimum. I hope that you enjoy these ideas and use them as a guide to develop your own special diet recipes for quick and delicious meals.

Planning Your Diet

The following recipes have been designed to fit low fat and low cholesterol diets. You will find that most of them are also low in sodium and require little refined sugar. Equally important, you will find that the microwave adapts readily to these types of diets, primarily because micro-cooking preserves the nutrients and flavor of foods.

Let's consider a few tips which seem to help generate a positive frame of mind for dieting. The right frame of mind towards changing eating habits is imperative. It greatly helps you to stay on a diet and to derive satisfaction from accomplished discipline. **Eventually a good frame of mind will allow you to enjoy your improved food program and a new self-image. Here are some tips:**

1. **Reduce your red meat consumption slowly over a month's time so that, ultimately, you eat red meat only once a week.** Red meat is a major source of fat and cholesterol in the American diet. Choose the less tender cuts of meat. They have less "marbling" (fat) and can be tenderized in a suitable marinade.

2. **Gradually reduce the amount of salt used in recipes or on your foods.** Use a salt substitute and just half the amount called for in a normal recipe. Use no salt when other condiments are used for seasoning. Your taste buds will adapt and you will become more aware of the natural taste of foods. Soon you will not miss the salt at all.

3. **When cooking with whole eggs, "dip out" half the yolk.** Use part of the egg shell to do the "dipping." This will instantly cut in half the cholesterol and fat content of the egg. In the diet recipes the term "dipped egg" will be used to denote this procedure.

4. **Drink non-fat milk and substitute a non-dairy creamer combined with non-fat milk to make "cream"** for cereals and fruits. The recipe is 1 part creamer to 7 parts non-fat milk.

160

5. **Eat foods with high water and fiber content.** Leafy vegetables, whole grain breads, cereals and fruits are good examples. For the same volume of food consumed, there will be far fewer calories and yet you will feel full.

6. **Fish is an excellent food.** Shellfish tend to be higher in cholesterol than fish. Limit shellfish to once a week in your diet.

7. **Eliminate foods made with a lot of refined sugar.** Eating refined sugar is like eating pure calories.

Now let's consider some actual recipes. I have provided main dishes (primarily fish and poultry), vegetables, desserts and breakfasts. Diet and enjoy it!

FISH—the following recipes can be enjoyed with a variety of fish. Try variations and come up with your own favorites. Sole, salmon, halibut, red snapper, cod, turbot and flounder are some good examples. Fish should look opaque and flake easily with a fork when cooked.

Don't over-cook. Remember that fish will after-cook. Allow fish to after-cook 5 minutes before serving.

Micro-cook on High power 5-7 minutes per pound. When micro-cooking a number of fish, alternate head and tail down the center of the dish or fold fillets in half with folded side to edge of dish.

MAIN DISHES—**many of the main dishes in this book are on the approved diet list. Simply omit the fat usually included in the regular recipe.** The microwave oven makes them quick and easy to prepare. Here are some other diet dishes to savor.

Savory Chili

1 lb. very lean ground beef (15% or less fat)	1 16 oz. can water-packed tomatoes
½ pkg. chili seasoning	1 6 oz. can tomato paste
1 medium onion, chopped	1 7¾ oz. can marinara sauce
1 27 oz. can red kidney beans	

1) Lightly coat a browning dish with a non-stick spray and pre-heat the dish on High power 6 minutes.
2) Break up ground beef on browning dish and micro-cook on High power 3-4 minutes until meat just loses its pinkness. Stir twice.
3) Add remaining ingredients, blend well and micro-cook on 50% power 15-18 minutes.

My cooking time _____

Lasagne Al Forno Special

3 cups tomato sauce	12 thin slices Mozzarella cheese
1 clove garlic, crushed	
½ teaspoon sweet basil	¼ cup fresh Parmesan cheese, grated (optional)
½ teaspoon oregano	
½ cup sunflower seeds, toasted	1 cup lowfat cottage cheese
1 bunch spinach	¾ lb. whole grain lasagne noodles

1) Cook noodles on conventional cooktop in boiling salted water 8-10 minutes until tender. Drain.
2) Crush garlic, sweet basil and oregano into tomato sauce.
3) Rinse spinach and shake leaves to remove excess water. Chop into bite-size pieces.
4) In a 3-quart dish spread ¾ cup of sauce, then ⅓ of noodles, ⅓ of spinach, ¼ of seeds, ¼ of cottage cheese and a layer of both cheeses. Repeat the layers of noodles, seeds and cheeses twice. Cover with remaining sauce and any remaining cheese and seeds.

5) Micro-cook on 70% power 6-8 minutes.
6) Allow to after-cook 15 minutes.

Tip: Sunflower seeds can be toasted on High power 5-7 minutes. Stir three times while toasting.

My cooking time _____

Simply Delicious Goulash   Serves 4–6

1 lb. ground meat
1 onion, chopped
2 cloves garlic, crushed
1 8 oz. can marinara sauce

1 8 oz. can tomato sauce
1 12 oz. pkg. large corkscrew
   macaroni

1) Preheat browning dish or grill for 6 minutes.
2) Crumble meat into dish and micro-cook on High power 2½-3½ minutes, stirring once.
3) Add onion and garlic. Micro-cook on High power 2 minutes more.
4) While meat mixture is cooking, *boil macaroni in a 3-quart sauce pan on conventional cooktop until macaroni is tender (5 to 8 minutes)*.
5) Drain macaroni.
6) Add sauces to meat and mix well.
7) Add drained macaroni to meat mixture and mix well.
8) Salt and pepper to taste. Micro-cook on High power 4-5 minutes.

My cooking time _____

Crispy Chicken   Serves 4

2½ lbs. chicken parts
2   egg whites, beaten
¼   cup non-fat milk

½ cup dry French bread
   crumbs
1 tablespoon seasoning salt
2 teaspoons brown sugar

Continued on next page   163

1) Combine egg whites and milk in a shallow dish. Blend well.
2) Combine dry ingredients and spread on a piece of wax paper.
3) Dip chicken parts in egg whites, then roll into crumb mixture.
4) Arrange chicken parts in a 2-quart dish, thicker parts to the edge of dish. Micro-cook on High power, covered with wax paper, 18-20 minutes.
5) Allow to after-cook 10 minutes.

My cooking time _____

Stuffed Roasting Hen

Serves 3-4

Chicken

1 4½ lb. whole fryer

Stuffing

¾	cup celery, chopped fine	⅛	teaspoon pepper
¼	cup onion, chopped fine	½	teaspoon dry thyme
2½	cups bread crumbs (3 slices)	¼	teaspoon sage
½	cup chicken bouillon	¼	teaspoon poultry seasoning

1) Place celery, onion and bouillon in 1-quart dish with lid. Micro-cook on High power 3-4 minutes.
2) Mix bread crumbs and seasonings into celery-onion mixture.
3) Rinse chicken and pat dry with paper towels. Stuff cavity and neck loosely with stuffing. Secure chicken with toothpicks, string or rubber band.
4) Sprinkle seasoned salt lightly over chicken. Place chicken breast side down on a microwave roasting rack in a 2-quart dish. Cover lightly with wax paper.
5) Micro-cook on High power 13 minutes. Turn chicken over and micro-cook on High power 12-13 minutes more until legs move easily.
6) Allow to after-cook while preparing sauce.

Soubise sauce

1	medium onion, sliced thin	1	envelope chicken broth with
¾	cup non-fat milk		seasonings
¼	cup water	½	teaspoon Kitchen Bouquet

7) Place onions in 1-quart dish with cover and micro-cook on High power 1½-2 minutes.
8) Add milk, water and chicken broth mix. Stir.
9) Micro-cook on High power 2-4 minutes more. Stir twice.
10) Allow to after-cook, covered, until slightly thickened. Stir and spoon over chicken. Serve remaining sauce in a sauceboat. Garnish chicken with orange slices or spiced peaches.

My cooking time _____

Fish-Vegetable Medley

Serves 2-3

1	lb. fish fillets, red snapper or	1	teaspoon lemon juice
	sole or halibut	½	cup soft bread crumbs
3	long slender carrots	2	teaspoons green onions,
1	chicken bouillon cube		chopped
¼	cup water	1	tablespoon parsley

1) Peel carrots. Wrap them in plastic film and micro-cook on High power 4-5 minutes until tender. Remove plastic. Set aside.
2) Cut fish into 3 even pieces.
3) Place water in 1-cup glass measure and boil on High power 45-60 seconds. Add bouillon cube and stir to dissolve.
4) Wrap fish fillets around carrots and secure with toothpicks. Be sure to let bright ends of carrots show.
5) Place in a 2-quart dish. Mix lemon juice in bouillon and pour over fish. Sprinkle with bread crumbs, onions and parsley. Cover with plastic film, venting one corner.
6) Micro-cook on High power 5-7 minutes until fish is opaque and flakes easily with a fork.
7) Allow to after-cook, covered, 5 minutes.

My cooking time _____

Peppy Sole

1 lb. sole fillets

1) Place sole in a 2-quart dish with lid. Set aside.

Sauce

⅓   cup chili sauce
1   tablespoon lemon juice
1   teaspoon prepared horseradish

1   teaspoon Worcestershire sauce
2   drops hot pepper sauce

2) Mix all ingredients well. Pour over fish. Micro-cook on High power 4-6 minutes, covered.
3) Allow to after-cook, covered, 5 minutes.

Tip: Excellent with fluffy rice.

My cooking time _____

Stuffed Salmon with Dill

Bread stuffing

¾   cup celery, chopped fine
¼   cup onion, chopped fine
2½ cups bread crumbs
½   cup chicken bouillon

⅛   teaspoon pepper
½   teaspoon dry thyme
½   teaspoon dill weed

1) Place celery, onion and bouillon in 1-quart dish with lid. Micro-cook on High power 3-4 minutes.
2) Mix bread crumbs and seasonings into celery-onion mixture. Set aside.

Salmon

2½ lbs. salmon
½   cup dry white wine

3) Rinse salmon and pat dry with paper towels.
4) Stuff salmon loosely with stuffing. Secure fish with toothpicks. Place fish in a large flat container and pour wine over all.
5) Cover and micro-cook on High power 12-14 minutes until fish flakes easily with a fork.
6) Allow to after-cook, covered, 5-10 minutes.

My cooking time _____

Patti's Red Snapper Special
Serves 6–8

Refer to this recipe in the Poultry and Fish section of this book. Substitute 2 tablespoons of water for the butter and olive oil.

In step 1, saute the onions and green pepper in the steam from the 2 tablespoons of water.

Poultry—especially moist and delicately delicious when micro-cooked. Be sure to skin it before serving.

Quick Chicken Breast
Serves 1

1 chicken breast, skinned
salt lightly

1) Place breast in a dish and cover with lid or plastic film.
2) Micro-cook on High power 4-6 minutes.
3) Allow to after-cook 5 minutes.

My cooking time _____

Zucchini Patty Special

Serves 4

2 cups coarsely grated
   zucchini
2-3 green onions, chopped
2 tablespoons fresh parsley
1 teaspoon basil
1 clove garlic, crushed
1 cup bread crumbs
¼ cup toasted sunflower seed
   meal

¼ teaspoon salt
¼ cup cooked rice or Bulgur
   grain
2 eggs, separated and yolks
   "dipped" (use the egg shell
   to "dip" out ½ of each yolk
   and discard that portion of
   the yolk)

1) Place the zucchini and onions in a 1-quart dish with lid. Micro-cook on High power 5-6 minutes.
2) Uncover dish, add parsley, then re-cover and allow parsley to wilt. (Dish outside of microwave oven.) When parsley wilts, add garlic and basil.
3) In a 2-quart dish, combine the sunflower seed meal, bread crumbs, rice and egg yolks. (Beat yolks slightly before adding.)
4) Add the zucchini-onion mixture and stir to blend well.
5) Beat the egg whites until stiff, then fold into zucchini mixture.
6) *Spray a skillet or grill with Pam. Preheat to hot.*
7) *Drop zucchini batter by spoonfuls into skillet and spread to form patties. Makes about 8 patties.*
8) Brown patties on both sides. (About 1-2 minutes per side.)

Tip: Patties can be reheated on platter in microwave oven. Leave space between patties, cover with paper towel. Use 70% power 2-3 minutes for 4 patties.

Tip: Sunflower meal can be made from sunflower seeds by grinding them to a fine crumb in food processor or blender. Micro-cook to toast on a flat plate 5-6 minutes on High power, stirring twice.

My cooking time _____

Vegetables. All the vegetables in the vegetable section of this book are acceptable for diets. Omit all butter or margarine and substitute 2 tablespoons of water to saute 1 quart of fresh vegetables. Don't add any water to those having a natural high water content, such as squash, potatoes and asparagus. You will find delectable flavors unique to each vegetable as your taste buds become accustomed to their natural goodness.

TIP: Vinaigrette type sauces often add titillating flavor to vegetables. Those sauces that have little or no oil are acceptable.

Rice cooks beautifully in the microwave oven, though you will save very little time. Use green onions, chives, curry, raisins, chicken bouillon or beef bouillon for flavoring. Season with pepper but omit the salt.

Long-grained rice requires 50% power. For Instant rice use High power. The following chart provides helpful tips.

Regular long-grain rice is dry grain which needs time to absorb water and soften.

High Power & 50% Power Long Grain Rice	2 servings	4 servings
Casserole	1-1½ qt.	2 qt.
Rice	½ cup	1 cup
Water	1 cup	2 cups
Start at High Power	3 minutes	5 minutes
Finish at 50% Power	8-10 minutes	11-15 minutes

High Power Quick-Cooking Rice	2 servings	4 servings
Casserole	1-1½ qt.	2 qt.
Rice	1 cup	2 cups
Water	¾ cup	1⅔ cups
High Power	2½-3½ minutes	6-8 minutes

Desserts. The goal when dieting is to enjoy desserts while using limited amounts of refined sugar. (The natural sugar found in fruits is all right.)

Poaching fruit is simple and the fruit is delicious when done in the microwave oven. Try the Poached Pears from the Desserts and Candy section. Brighten and sweeten fruits with the Raspberry Sauce from the Sauce section. Use 1 tablespoon per serving.

Continued on next page

TIP: To sweeten desserts, use powdered sugar instead of granulated sugar to sprinkle on top.

Baked Apples: Pare around the stem of apple core. Place in dish with lid or use plastic film for a cover. Micro-cook on High power in accordance with following table:

Number Apples	Brown Sugar (teaspoon)	Cinnamon (teaspoon)	Red Candies	Raisins	Time (minutes)
1	½	dash	2	1 tablespoon	3-4
2	1	¼	4	2 tablespoons	4-6
4	2	½	8	⅓ cup	6-8
6	3	½	12	½ cup	8-10

Puddings:

Quick and delicious right in the bowl or serving dish. Use non-fat milk. Stir frequently after the first 3 minutes. Use High power.

Vanilla & Tapioca Mixes	Non-fat Milk	Time
3¼ oz. package	2 cups	6-7 minutes
2 pkgs. each 3¼ oz.	4 cups	12-13 minutes
5¼ oz. package	3 cups	9-10 minutes

BREAKFAST SUGGESTIONS:

En Concert Super Lowfat Hash Browns

Micro-cook potatoes according to chart in Quick Tips section.

When potatoes have cooled, cut up and spread in a pre-heated conventional skillet that has been coated with non-stick vegetable spray.

Add 1 teaspoon butter for each large potato. Season with chopped onion and pepper to taste. Add a dash of salt. Brown until golden.

Lowfat bacon

Micro-cook bacon according to chart in Quick Tips section. Micro-cook on several paper towels. Allow to after-cook, then cut off fatty parts.

"Dipped" Scrambled Eggs

Use egg shell to "dip out" half of yolk. Micro-cook on 70% power, covered. Stir eggs from outside edge toward middle while cooking. Remove eggs from microwave oven while they still look "damp." Keep eggs covered while they after-cook.

Number Dipped Eggs	Non-fat Milk	Chives	Crumbled Bacon (pieces)	Time
1	—	½ teaspoon	1	40-55 seconds
2	1 tablespoon	1 teaspoon	1½	77-70 seconds
4	2 tablespoons	1 tablespoon	3	1½-2½ minutes
6	¼ cup	1 tablespoon	5	3-4 minutes
10	½ cup	2 tablespoons	7	5-6 minutes

Recommended allowance—two "dipped" eggs per week, per person.

Cereals

Cereals are delicious in seconds in the microwave oven. All ingredients are added in the beginning and stirred once during cooking. Washing up is easy as the cereal does not stick to the dish.

For cream, use 1 part non-dairy creamer to 7 parts non-fat milk.

The following chart provides helpful cooking tips:

High Power Quick Oatmeal	1 serving	2 servings	4 servings
Bowl Size	1 qt.	1-1½ qt.	2 qt.
Cereal	⅓ cup	⅔ cup	1⅓ cups
Water	¾ cup	1½ cups	3 cups
Time	2-2½ min.	4-5 min.	6-7 min.

Old Fashioned Oatmeal	1 serving	2 servings	4 servings
Bowl Size	1 qt.	1-1½ qt.	2 qt.
Cereal	⅓ cup	⅔ cup	1⅓ cups
Water	¾ cup	1⅓ cups	2½ cups
Time	4-6 min.	5-7 min.	8-9 min.

Continued on next page   171

Instant Cream of Wheat	1 serving	2 servings	4 servings
Bowl Size	1 qt.	2 qt.	3 qt.
Cereal	2½ tbsps.	⅓ cup	⅔ cup
Water	¾ cup	1⅓ cups	2¾ cups
Time	1½-2½ min.	2½-3½ min.	4½-6 min.

Regular Cream of Wheat	1 serving	2 servings	4 servings
Bowl Size	1 qt.	2 qt.	3 qt.
Cereal	2½ tbsps.	⅓ cup	⅔ cup
Water	1 cup	1¾ cups	3½ cups
Time	4-6 min.	5½-7½ min.	9-12 min.

Quick Tips

Planning your cooking sequence

As you know, the microwave oven cooks food internally by creating very rapid molecular motion within the food. **The cooking effect of microwaves does not stop when the cooking cycle is complete, but rather continues for some period of time, depending upon the type of food being cooked.** I call this "after-cooking" and I allow for it in all my recipes. This will be important when planning your cooking sequence.

Therefore, as you make menu plans, consider the two aspects of timing foods cooked in the microwave oven; the actual time in the microwave oven and the after-cooking time. This is when you should remember to take advantage of being able to cook food ahead of time and reheat it just before serving. You can do this with no loss of quality or taste.

This is especially important when cooking for more than eight people. For instance, potatoes of all kinds are excellent when reheated. Why not cook them earlier in the day and refrigerate them until dinner? Allow a few seconds more for reheating whole potatoes and be sure to fluff the mashed potatoes once during reheating for more even penetration of the microwave energy. Fresh vegetables can also be cooked earlier and reheated beautifully.

With a little pre-planning, any large meal can be a lot less work and you can have even more variety in your menus when using your microwave oven *en concert* with your other cooking appliances.

Continued on next page

A turkey takes only 7-7½ minutes per pound in the microwave oven, so a 14-pound stuffed bird can be cooked in just one hour and 40 minutes, will after-cook for 20 minutes and is ready to be carved in just two hours from start to finish!

Planning is of utmost importance, therefore. Analyze your menu and decide which dishes you prefer to cook conventionally and which ones are better done in the microwave oven. Suppose you are planning to serve both a ham and a large turkey. The turkey (over 14 pounds) may be easier to roast conventionally while the ham and vegetables can be cooked more easily in the microwave oven with the added advantage of only one pan to clean.

An excellent way to make pies which call for a pre-baked crust is to make the filling in a mixing bowl in the microwave oven while you bake the crust conventionally.

Suppose you are planning a dinner of roast beef, baked potatoes, frozen peas, salad, rolls and pudding. All the cooking can be done in the microwave oven. The sequence of preparation and the timing would be:

	Cooking Time	After-cooking Time
1. Tapioca Pudding— 3¼ oz. package	5½-6½ minutes	30-60 seconds
2. 4-lb. Beef Roast— Room temperature	28 minutes	15 minutes
3. Fix salad and set table.	None	None
4. Scrub and pierce potatoes- 1 medium potato 2 medium potatoes 3 medium potatoes 4 medium potatoes 5 medium potatoes 6 medium potatoes	5 minutes 9 minutes 12 minutes 15 minutes 18 minutes 20 minutes	5 minutes or more for all quantities
5. 1 package frozen peas	5 minutes	Serve immediately
6. Rolls—8 in a basket	15-30 seconds	None

Since the pudding must cool and can be made ahead of time, it is to be done first (perhaps in the morning). To allow for the after-cooking, you will start the roast about 45 minutes before you plan to serve dinner. Make the salad and set the table while the meat is cooking. The potatoes go in as the roast comes out and they will be done just in time to after-cook while the peas are cooking. The rolls can heat as you serve dinner.

Breakfast or brunch can be a feast done in record time. Your menu may consist of grapefruit, "zippy" hash browns, scrambled eggs, bacon and coffee cake. This is an *en concert* menu because the eggs can be cooked conventionally while the bacon is in the microwave oven. The sequence of preparation and the timing is:

	Cooking Time	After-cooking Time
1. Potatoes 3 large	12 to 15 minutes	5 to 15 minutes
2. Coffee cake	5½ to 6 minutes	10 to 15 minutes
3. Cut grapefruit, set table	None	None
4. Cook bacon, 8 pieces	5 to 5½ minutes	None
5. Scramble eggs, 4 eggs	2½ to 3 minutes	A few seconds

The potatoes can be cooked the night before or you can do them in the morning. While the potatoes are cooking, mix the coffee cake. After the potatoes are done, remove them from the microwave oven and put in the coffee cake. As the cake is cooking, hash-brown the potatoes on your cooktop. When the coffee cake is ready, replace it with the bacon. While the cake is after-cooking, scramble the eggs on the cooktop. This *en concert* breakfast is ready for a family of 4 in less than 30 minutes.

Adapting Your Own Recipes to the Microwave Oven

No matter what type of cooking you like, many of your favorite recipes can be prepared in the microwave oven. **Refer to a similar recipe from this book or another microwave cookbook and follow**

Continued on next page   175

the general guidelines for the type of food involved.

The first time you try a recipe, check the food after it has micro-cooked 2 minutes, then rotate the container or stir the food. Check it again in another 2 minutes. At this time you should get an idea of how close it is to being done. Remember to allow for after-cooking! Make a note of the time in the space provided in this book or in your conventional cookbook. Next time you will know exactly.

When cooking on High power, it will take about one-fourth the time conventional cooking takes. For instance, the Sweet Potato Soufflé in this book takes one hour when cooked conventionally, but only 10 minutes plus 5 minutes after-cooking when a microwave oven is used.

If the food to be cooked in the microwave oven produces a large quantity of its own juices, reduce by one-half the amount of liquid that you put into the microwave oven. Microwave energy is attracted to liquid, so an excess will slow the cooking time. Microwave cooking requires very little liquid since the food will not dehydrate in the microwave oven unless the food is overcooked.

Casseroles with an uncooked rice base will take a bit longer than one-fourth their conventional cooking time, for the rice must absorb the liquid. Try using precooked rice for fast results. Whenever you cook rice conventionally, double the recipe and save the excess in the refrigerator to use in casseroles later.

Foods From the Freezer and New Tips on Defrosting

The simplicity of defrosting foods in a microwave oven is one of its most useful assets. You can prepare foods from the freezer in a very short time. **Many companies cover defrosting very adequately in their microwave oven instruction books.** The following basic principles are good to remember for all brands and models of microwave ovens:

Some microwave ovens have a special button or dial position for defrosting, sometimes labeled "Defrost." In this position the oven cycles on and off. For instance, the oven may be on for 30 seconds and then off for 30 seconds when "Defrost" is selected. **This process will slow the heating of the food and allow time for the temperature to equalize throughout the food.**

Meats. You must allow time for roasts and other large pieces of meat to defrost completely and to equalize the temperature throughout the meat. Remember, the microwave energy decreases rapidly every ¾ inch of food it penetrates, so partially fro-

zen meat or food that is room temperature on the outside and extremely cold on the inside will not cook well.

Hamburger defrosts quickly, usually 5 to 6 minutes per pound. **To avoid cooked spots while defrosting, turn the meat over and around after 3½ minutes and remove any defrosted portion.**

Chops and steaks are done in the same manner as hamburger. Stack the chops or steaks in the microwave oven and alternate the packages or meat when resetting your timer or checking on the defrosting. Six chops or two steaks will defrost in 10 to 14 minutes total time, during which the microwave oven will be on for 5 to 7 minutes. Remember, after-cooking occurs after defrosting too, so allow the temperature of the meat to equalize for a few minutes before starting the cooking process.

Bacon. One pound of bacon takes 30-45 seconds on High power to be able to separate slices.

Vegetables. Vegetables can be cooked directly from the frozen state, with no defrosting. It is not necessary to add water as the frozen crystals will provide enough water. Cook them in their pouch or box but be sure to puncture the pouch 3 or 4 times and shake it after 3 minutes of cooking. This helps the cooking to be even and is particularly necessary for mixed vegetables. **Cooking times for specific vegetables are given in the Vegetables Chapter.**

Casseroles. A four-cup casserole with a noodle or cooked rice and meat base will defrost in 6 to 8 minutes total time, during which the microwave oven will be on 3 to 4 minutes. Allow the casserole to after-cook for 5 to 10 minutes, then heat in the microwave oven for 3 to 4 minutes, rotating the container after 2 minutes. Casserole will be ready from freezer to table in just 14 to 16 minutes.

Rolls and Bread. REMOVE ANY WIRE TWISTS FROM THE PACKAGE. A dozen rolls will be ready in just 1¼ minutes. Open the plastic bag to allow steam to escape and insert one or two paper napkins to absorb extra water crystals.

French rolls are delicious if you don't overdo them. One French roll from frozen state takes 30 seconds on High power. For two or more rolls, stack them by two's near the center. Eight rolls will take 1 to 1½ minutes.

Four slices of frozen bread when stacked take 30 seconds on High power. You can use the few minutes of after-cooking to make sandwiches. They will be ready to eat by the time you finish.

Continued on next page   177

To defrost frozen bread dough from the grocery store, place two frozen loaves in a 2-quart utility dish on a microwave roasting rack. Add 1 cup warm water to dish. Defrost on 10% power 30 minutes. Shape dough as desired. Place in warm conventional oven to finish rising.

Vegetables

The texture and color retention of vegetables cooked in the microwave oven is far superior to most conventional ways of cooking. For best results follow these two basic rules:

Use a container with a well-fitted lid or cover the container with plastic film. The microwave oven does not dehydrate foods, therefore you will be cooking with very little moisture. This results in excellent nutrition and taste but it means that evaporation must be controlled. Cooking bags are just right for this. If you seal the bags, puncture 3 or 4 holes for the steam to escape.

Stir vegetables at least once while cooking to permit even cooking throughout. Vegetables have almost no after-cooking so they are ready to eat immediately.

When micro-cooking fresh vegetables, use no more than two tablespoons of water to one quart of vegetables; three to four tablespoons for two quarts.

Table of Typical Cooking Times for Potatoes
(After-cooking time is at least 5 minutes for all quantities.)

Number Potatoes	Cooking Time	Tip	My Time Cooking/ After-cooking
1 medium	5 minutes	Rub butter or bacon grease on skin to obtain crispy finish.	___|___
2 medium	9 minutes	Placing potatoes on a microwave roasting rack allows more even cooking and eliminates rotating.	___|___
3 medium	12 minutes	When cooking one potato, place in	___|___
4 medium	15 minutes	center of microwave oven. When cooking more than one, space evenly. Three or more, space in spoke pattern.	___|___
5 medium	18 minutes	Select evenly shaped potatoes for more even cooking.	___|___
6 medium	20 minutes	Sweet potatoes take 1 minute less per potato than Irish potatoes.	___|___

Frozen Food Timing Table

Frozen Vegetable	Cooking Time	Tip	My Cooking Time
Broccoli	6 minutes	Cook all frozen vegetables in pouch or box after puncturing the pouch 3 to 4 times; shake after 2½ to 3 minutes.	_____
Carrots, cut	5½-6½ minutes		_____
Cauliflower	6 minutes		_____
Cut Corn	5½-6 minutes		_____
Peas	5 minutes		_____
Squash	6 minutes		_____
Mixed Vegetables	5½-6½ minutes		_____
Corn-on-the-cob	2½-3 minutes per cob	Cook in plastic film or plastic bag from store, puncture bag	_____
Vegetables, with Sauce	5½-6½ minutes	Put in covered container; stir after 3 minutes	_____
Dense vegetables such as baby Lima Beans	6-7 minutes	Put in covered container with 2 tablespoons water; stir after 3 minutes	_____

Meats and Poultry

Many meats can be cooked very nicely in the microwave oven with an amazing savings in time. Here are some general principles for micro-cooking meats and poultry:

Large cuts of meat. Select cuts that are as even in diameter as possible. Make sure that the temperature is even throughout the meat before starting to micro-cook it. Remember that microwave energy loses strength every ¾ inch of food penetration and meat that is cold in the center will not cook as rapidly as the outer meat.

Cover meat with a paper towel while cooking to retard spatter and absorb excess moisture.

When micro-cooking on High power, turn large cuts of meat over and around every 10 minutes. Drain off excess juices since they attract microwave energy and slow cooking times. Add seasonings after the first 20 minutes of micro-cooking.

Less tender cuts. Any rapid cooking tends to toughen meat fibers. There are several ways, however, to use your microwave oven with less tender (and less expensive) meats and still obtain quick cooking and tenderness:

Marinate the meats. Use your favorite marinade or a commercial tenderizer for at least an hour and preferably longer.

Use a tenderizer, such as wine, when micro-cooking meats.

Cook meats in a cooking bag when possible. Cook on 30% power or Defrost setting.

Smaller cuts—since smaller cuts of meat cook extremely fast, it is important to use a favorite seasoning to add color and eye appeal or use a browning dish, if you have one. It is also easy to slip the meat under the broiler for a minute or two to achieve a crispy, brown exterior.

Before defrosting meat, remove plastic film. The film creates an uneven heat pattern and will tend to cook some portions of the meat.

If a browning dish or grill is to be pre-heated, leave the lid off and pre-heat on High power 5-6 minutes for maximum heat penetration.

If meat is at refrigerator temperature and is going to be placed directly on a hot browning dish, warm meat on 30% power 2-3 minutes, then pat meat with paper towel before placing it on pre-heated browning dish.

Continued on next page   181

Table of Typical Cooking Times for Meats

Meats, tender cuts	Power Setting	Cooking Time per Pound
Beef, Roast Medium		
Room Temperature	High	7-7½ minutes
Refrigerator temperature	High	7½-8 minutes
Just defrosted	High	8-8½ minutes
Less tender cuts	30%	12-14 minutes
Ham, uncooked	70%	9-10 minutes
precooked	70%	4-5 minutes
Pork roast, cold	70%	9-10 minutes
Hamburger Patties, ¼ lb.	High	1-2 minutes
Hamburgers in buns		
4 hamburgers, stack 2 on 2	High	30 seconds to heat
Hot dog in bun	High	30 seconds for one
4 hot dogs	High	1½ minutes for hot dogs, then put in buns and cook 30 seconds more
Bacon, 1 piece, crisp	High	75 seconds
very crisp	High	90 seconds
4 pieces	High	3 minutes
6 pieces	High	4-4½ minutes
8 pieces	High	5-6 minutes

Table of Typical Cooking Times for Poultry

		Power Setting	Cooking Time per Pound
Chicken breast, ½ large	One	High	4½ minutes
	Two	High	7½-8 minutes
Chicken, whole		High	5-6 minutes
Turkey, cold		High	7-8 minutes
Turkey, roast, rolled (7 pounds)		High	5-6 minutes

Table of Cooking Times (Continued)

My Time Cooking/After-cooking	Tip
	Turn every 10 minutes
	Turn or stir twice
	Cover with paper towel; turn every 10 minutes; put on glaze the last 10 minutes; after-cook 15 minutes
	Select roast with even diameter; drain juice after first half of cooking time
	Turn after 1 minute; use browning dish or color with Kitchen Bouquet or soy sauce
	Cook patties first, then put them into buns and warm together
	Heat hot dogs and buns separately if preparing more than one
	Buns will be warm, not leathery
	Cook on paper plates; stack bacon in 3 layers, 3 pieces to a layer with paper towel between layers. With more than 2 layers, use a folded piece of newsprint between paper towels

Table of Cooking Times (Continued)

My Time Cooking/After-cooking	Tip
	Turn after 3 minutes; use browning dish, Shake-N-Bake or finish in broiler
	Use favorite packaged seasoning or browning dish to brown all sides
	Turn every 20 minutes for 10-14 pounds; every 15 minutes for 6-8 pounds
	Defrost before cooking, preferably night before; cover with paper towel; rotate every 12 minutes; after-cook 10 minutes

Breads

Breads take very little time to micro-cook or to be reheated in the Microwave oven. **CAUTION: Bread left in the microwave oven too long becomes hard and leathery.**

"Day-Old" Breads. Put a small container of water in the corner of the microwave oven. Use a cheese or shot glass with about ¾ inch of water in it. The water will absorb some of the microwave energy but the steam from the water will have a positive effect on breads and rolls.

Breakfast rolls—heating time: Fresh rolls—8 to 10 seconds on High or Reheat setting.

Slightly dry rolls—spray lightly with water and heat 10 to 15 seconds on High.

Very dry rolls—place a glass container with ¾ inch water in it in a corner of microwave oven. Set timer to:
15 seconds for 1 roll
20 seconds for 2 rolls
30 seconds for 3 rolls

Dinner Rolls. Warm rolls right in the basket you will use on the table. For 8 to 10 fresh dinner rolls, 30 seconds is usually right. If they are especially large, they may take 45 seconds.

If rolls are taken directly from the freezer, remove any metal twist-tie and insert two unfolded paper napkins in and around rolls. This will absorb the water crystals and keep the rolls from becoming soggy. Heat 8 to 10 frozen rolls on High power 20 seconds. Jiggle rolls in the napkins and heat on High power 10-15 seconds more. Serve immediately.

French Bread. Heat in a brown paper bag that has been sprinkled lightly with water. The water adds just a bit of steam to attract some of the microwave energy and results in delicious, warm French bread. Warm a half-loaf in just 30 seconds.

Frozen Bread. Stack and thaw 4 pieces at a time. It takes just 30 seconds. Let bread finish defrosting as you make the sandwiches or as you put it on the table.

Reheating Foods

One of the most amazing qualities about microwave cooking is its ability to keep food from dehydrating and tasting "left-over".

You can regulate the moisture content of pre-cooked or frozen foods. You will find that foods almost never dehydrate, and that you can actually revitalize many foods which you normally would have thrown out.

Reheating Foods General. Almost all foods can be reheated in a microwave oven. **The same principles that affect timing in the initial cooking also affect reheating times.** The starting temperature, moisture content, density and quantity of food should all be considered. **In general, reheating one serving takes 15 to 30 seconds less if it starts at room temperature.** Each additional serving will add 30 to 45 seconds to the reheating time.

"Dry Foods" Put a small container of water in the corner of the microwave oven. Use a cheese glass or shot glass with about ¾ inch of water in it. **The water will absorb some of the microwave energy but the steam from the water will have a positive effect on dry foods such as French bread, "stale" breakfast rolls and acorn squash.**

Meat and Poultry. A large platter of sliced meat can be reheated in 3 to 4 minutes. **Cover the meat with a plastic film and rotate the container after 2 minutes. If there seems to be more moisture than you like, put a layer of paper towels under the plastic film.** The paper will absorb some of the moisture giving the meat a crisp, dry texture.

Vegetables. Left-over vegetables are delicious even if you are reheating just one serving. **Use a container that comfortably holds the amount of vegetables you are reheating, put 1 teaspoon of water in the container for each cup of vegetables and cover the vegetables with tight fitting lid or plastic film.** Stir after 2 minutes. Two cups will reheat in 2 to 3 minutes.

Rice reheats beautifully when taken directly from the freezer. Two cups of cooked, frozen rice will heat in 4 to 5 minutes.

Breads, Waffles, Pancakes. Breakfast breads can be made ahead of time and reheated for late sleepers (even if the cook is the late sleeper). **Stack them to retard the energy penetration and put them in the microwave oven.** Three pancakes, waffles or pieces of French toast will take 20 to 30 seconds, if taken right from the refrigerator. If you take them directly from the freezer, use paper towels

Continued on next page   185

between them to absorb excess moisture and wrap them *lightly* in plastic film. They will take 45 to 60 seconds to heat.

One breakfast roll takes only 5 to 7 seconds. **Don't heat breads too long. They will get leathery.** The old-fashioned method of putting breads in a brown bag to warm comes in handy here. Put them in the bag and sprinkle the bag with water. You can heat 4 to 5 rolls in 30 seconds.

Coffee. One freshly-made pot will last all day. Perk it or make a filter pot, but don't keep it hot. Just leave the pot on the counter. When you are ready, pour the coffee into a cup and place cup inside the microwave oven for 1 minute 15 seconds.

Stuffing. Add about 2 tablespoons of water to each 4 cups of stuffing. Cover and stir after 1 minute. It will take 2 to 3 minutes to heat.

Gravy and Sauces. For 1½ to 2 cups, heat for 2 to 2½ minutes. Stir after 60 seconds.

Baby Food

The microwave oven is ideal for heating baby foods. It is fast and there is no clean-up.

8 oz. bottle—from refrigerator, High power 1-1½ minutes; room temperature, High power 45-60 seconds

Meat mixed with vegetables—from refrigerator, High power 45-60 seconds; room temperature, High power 30-45 seconds

Cereal mixed with fruit and milk—High power 45-60 seconds

Fruit alone—High power 30-45 seconds

General Tips

Browning meats: Roasts with little or no outer fat, such as eye of round or veal roasts, will not brown as nicely as those that have a nice layer of fat. Make your own fat layer by using bacon strips side by side secured in place by wooden toothpicks.

Dilute 1 tablespoon of Kitchen Bouquet, or other favorite dark seasoning, with 1 tablespoon of water and brush on roast after it has been cooking for 20 minutes or so.

When seasoning a roast, lightly sprinkle the meat with a little white or brown sugar. This will give a light glazed appearance. This is especially good with pork roast.

Chocolate Curls: To curl chocolate, warm a 2-oz. bar on 70% power 15 seconds. Use a vegetable peeler with long narrow blade to draw long chocolate curls. Draw curls from top for wide curls and from edge for narrow curls.

Chocolate—melting: Use a glass container. For 2 squares of 1 oz. each, heat 60 seconds on High or 1 minute 30 seconds on Roast power, or 70%.

Coffee—reheating: Coffee may be reheated up to four times and still taste fresh! One 8 oz. cup of coffee takes 1 minute 15 seconds on High.

Instant coffee—place instant coffee into cold water in a cup. Heat for 1 minute 30 seconds to 2 minutes on High.

Eggs—poached: Always start cooking with very hot water. After slipping egg into the water, puncture the egg with a toothpick to eliminate any chance of it bursting. Cook on High:

1 egg for 45-60 seconds
2 eggs for 1¼-1½ minutes
4 eggs for 1½-2½ minutes

Let egg(s) after-cook for a few seconds then lift onto a piece of toast with a slotted spoon.

Eggs—scrambled: Remember the SECOND KEY TO SUCCESS, After-cooking! Remove the eggs from the microwave oven when they still look damp, fluff with a fork and serve. (The eggs will continue to cook for some seconds.) Use 70% power to scramble eggs.

Eggs	Milk	Butter	Time
1	1 tablespoon	—	45-60 seconds
2	2 tablespoons	1 teaspoon	60-75 seconds
4	2 tablespoons	2 teaspoons	2-3 minutes
6	¼ cup	1 tablespoon	3¼-4¼ minutes
10	½ cup	2 tablespoons	5¼-6½ minutes

Egg—whites: To bring egg whites to room temperature quickly, place in a glass measure. Warm on High power 10-12 seconds.

Foil or Shielding: Metal or foil has the property of totally reflecting microwave energy. Because of this property, foil can be used to great advantage. It is called shielding. Remember this rule—Never cover more than one fourth of the food mass with foil. This will allow the energy to bounce off the shield and into the exposed food. Do not let the foil touch the bottom or sides of the microwave oven.

Continued on next page

Fresh greens: To keep greens fresh and crisp, rinse well and shake off excess water. Lay greens on paper toweling and roll up toweling. Place in plastic bag and refrigerate.

Corn on the Cob: Cook right in the plastic film or plastic bag from the store. Puncture a hole in the bag first.

Gravy: Save the juice drained from canned vegetables for making gravy or sauce. Use juice in place of water.

Lemon juice: To get maximum juice from a lemon, heat the lemon in microwave oven on High power for 1 minute before squeezing.

Meringue: To get the egg whites to room temperature quickly, place the whites in a glass measure and heat in a microwave oven:
    2 egg whites for 8 to 10 seconds
    3 egg whites for 10 to 12 seconds
To bake the meringue, place pie in microwave oven and cook for 2 to 4 minutes, rotating the pie dish several times. Test for doneness with wooden toothpick. DO NOT OVERCOOK! After meringue is cooked, sprinkle with toasted slivered almonds for color.

Poultry: A 6 to 8 pound turkey is delicious when cooked in a microwave oven but is not as eye-appealing as we might like:
    Brush the bird with a little margarine or salad oil after it has been cooked and place it under a pre-heated broiler for 2 to 4 minutes. (This works well for chicken too.)

Rice-A Roni: In a 10″ glass baking dish melt 2 tablespoons of butter or margarine until sizzling hot. Use High power 2-3 minutes. Pour in vermicelli mixture. Stir to spread evenly. Micro-cook on High power 2-3 minutes until golden. Stir twice to spread evenly.
    Add 2 cups of hot water, stir and add sauce mixture. Stir again. Cover baking dish and micro-cook on 70% power 12-14 minutes. Stir 2-3 times while cooking. Allow to after-cook, covered, 5 minutes.

Noodle Roni, parmesáno: Cook noodles as directed on package. Drain.
    In a 2-quart casserole dish with lid, warm ½ cup milk and 2 tablespoons butter on High power 60 seconds. Stir in sauce mixture. Mix thoroughly. Pour in drained noodles. Toss to coat noodles well. Micro-cook, covered, on 70% power 60 seconds more.

Noodle Roni Supréma: Cook noodles as directed on package. Drain.
    In a 2-quart casserole dish with lid, melt 2 tablespoons of butter or

margarine on High power 20-30 seconds. Break in 2 eggs, stir with fork and micro-cook on 70% power 1-1½ minutes. Stir in ½ cup milk and 1 tablespoon white wine. Stir parmesáno sauce into mixture, then toss noodles gently into sauce. Micro-cook, covered, on 70% power 60 seconds more.

Removing odors from microwave oven: In a small glass container mix 5 to 6 tablespoons of lemon juice with an equal amount of water. Heat in microwave oven for 2 minutes on High power.

Defrosting frozen fruit: For 16 oz. boxes of fruit, remove metal lid from box and place the box of fruit in a small bowl. Heat for 2½ minutes on High power then use a fork to break fruit apart. Let after-cook a few seconds and serve.

To toast nuts: Place ½ cup of nuts in a glass pie plate and micro-cook on High power 5-7 minutes, stirring three times while cooking.

To shell walnuts: Place 1 cup of walnuts and 1 cup of water in a 2 cup glass measure. Heat for 1 minute 30 seconds to 2 minutes on High power. Drain off water and crack walnuts.

To soften butter: Heat for 12 seconds on High power or 60 seconds on Warm.

To melt butter: Melt butter right in the dish you plan to use or in any suitable container. The times below are based on High power.

Amount	Time
2 tablespoons	20-30 seconds
¼ cup	45-60 seconds
½ cup	60-90 seconds
¾ cup	1½-2½ minutes

To soften cream cheese: For 4 oz. heat 30 seconds on High power or 60 seconds on Warm.

For 8 oz. heat 60 seconds on High power or 2 minutes on Warm power.

Continued on next page   189

To heat or scald milk: Microwave energy is attracted to liquid, fat and sugar. The amount of fat in milk will make a slight difference in the heating time. For example; one cup of non-fat milk will take 30-45 seconds longer to scald than one cup of homogenized milk. The times in this chart are based on homogenized milk and High power.

Amount	To Warm	To Scald
½ cup	30-45 seconds	45-60 seconds
1 cup	45-60 seconds	60-75 seconds
1½ cups	1-1½ minutes	1½-2 minutes

Squash: When cooking squash without a container, place a glass with ½ to ¾ inch of water in it in a corner of the microwave oven to add a little moisture.

Vegetables: Cook all frozen vegetables in pouch or box after puncturing the container 2 to 4 times. Shake the container after 2½ to 3 minutes of cooking time.

Warming brandy for flambé: Remove top from bottle of brandy and place in microwave oven for 1½ to 2 minutes on High setting.

Yeast breads: Use a 4 cup glass measure instead of a saucepan and warm ingredients initially in microwave oven for 1 to 2 minutes on High power, then add ingredients to the flour and yeast mixture.

Microwave Heat Probe Reference Table

Many microwave ovens have an optional automatic temperature probe. The probe connects to the microwave oven and is inserted in the food to be cooked. The cooking time is determined by pre-selecting a final temperature on the microwave oven front.

If your microwave oven is a model that has this convenience, you will find this chart helpful in selecting the proper degree of heat to set for micro-cooking various foods. The probe will turn the microwave oven off when the pre-selected temperature is reached. .

Temperature	Typical Dish
185°	Ham Loaf
175°	Stuffed Peppers (with raw ground beef)
170°	Hot Coffee, Vegetable Casseroles (with frozen vegetables)
140°-145°	Roast Beef (well-done) Remember, temperature will rise 15°-20° while after-cooking.
160°	Stews, Chunky Soups, Poached Fruits
155°	Heating Casseroles
150°	Canned Foods, Reheating Leftovers, Defrosting Convenience Foods
140°	Creamed Soups
130°-135°	Roast Beef (medium) Remember, temperature will rise 15°-20° while after-cooking.
135°	Leg of Lamb (medium)
130°	Cheese Dips, Warming Beverages or Breakfast Syrups
125°	Roast Beef (rare)
120°	Reheat Pies, Fruit Compotes or Desserts
115°	Heat Canned Ham
110°	Heating Cheese or Meat Sandwich
90°	Heating Sour Cream Dips

Do's

Cook the minimum time, test, then cook some more if necessary.

Test the cooking container if in doubt of its usability.

Use a string to tie roasts, turkey legs, etc., together.

When using a built-in "browner," make sure the cooking container can withstand the heat.

Space food evenly within the microwave oven.

Keep door and seal clean of food and crumbs.

In older homes, use a separate electric circuit for the microwave oven.

Don'ts

Use a metal cooking container.

Use a china cooking container with a metal rim.

Operate the microwave oven when it is empty.

Slam or mistreat the door.

Use any metal twists such as those often found on plastic or paper bags.

Cover more than one-fourth of food mass with foil.

Use a container that is large at the top and small at the bottom.

Index

194